Limitless

Escape The Rat Race and Make Money Online in the New Economy

Work From Anywhere You Want Using
'HTAM' - A New Business Model That Has
Helped Regular People Earn A
Documented $51 Million To Date

Matt Lloyd

Founder and President of MOBE,
The Leading Online Business Education Company

CONTENTS

Acknowledgments

In late 2008, I made a decision that would transform my financial life forever. It would allow me to go from a life constrained by a lack of money to one where I am completely free to do what I want, when I want, and with whom I want. A life where on a whim, I can book a first class ticket to the island of Fiji and arrive on its beaches the next day. A life where the phrase *"I can't afford it"* is no longer part of my vocabulary. A life where I had, for the first time ever, *real freedom*. That one seemingly small decision was the catalyst for a business that has paid out over $51 million in commissions to people around the world, changing their lives forever.

That's how powerful decisions can be. You may not believe me just yet, but your decision to buy this book was one of the best you've ever made for your financial future.

Even though I have given myself just 30 hours to write the entire first draft of this book, it has been years in the making. I've literally travelled the world gathering the knowledge and experiences you'll soon read about. There's no way I could ever have done it on my own. As clichéd as it sounds—and remember, things become clichés because they have a core of truth—I have an enormous list of people to thank.

The first are my parents. To this day, they still work the farm that I was raised on, growing wheat and raising sheep. My father taught me the value of hard work. Even now, in his 60s, he's capable of working 18 hours straight when the farm is busy (sleeping in the paddock when needed), putting most 20 year olds to shame with his work ethic. He taught me that, when running your business, you should aim to accomplish at least one thing that's significant every day.

My mother taught me the value of doing the right thing, being kind to others, and remaining humble. She only ever offered me encouragement, and believed in me more than anyone else.

Both encouraged my childhood business ventures, as crazy as they seemed, and gave me solid foundations in life.

I also owe a lot to the MOBE staff team. As of the time of writing, we have over 185 staff members spread around the world (we're predominantly a virtual organization, where our staff work online from home) who help me handle everything: running our live events, keeping existing websites up and running, creating new website and product designs, finding new business, coaching clients, handling phone sales, coming up with new programs, answering customer service tickets, making travel arrangements, crafting my last-minute sales presentations, and about 1,000 other essential tasks. There are a lot of moving parts to running a company like MOBE. As the face of the business, I usually get all the credit and accolades—but the majority of it should go to the team behind me. If you're on that team and reading this right now, *thank you*. I appreciate your support, hard work, loyalty, and for believing in MOBE's mission.

I'm also grateful for every single MOBE affiliate, from the top-grossing heavy hitters right down to the newbies who just started and haven't yet earned their first commissions. You folks keep the dream alive, and never fail to find new ways to amaze me. At the time of writing, MOBE has created over $100 million in revenue. The truth is, without the help of our affiliates (who received a large share of that $100 million), MOBE wouldn't have done even a third of that amount. A big special thanks to the highest paid affiliates, some of whom have become millionaires (in U.S. dollars) from their MOBE efforts alone.

In order of the total amount of income earned, a special thanks goes to:

Darren Salkeld

Tim Donovan

Shaqir Hussyin

Paul Lynch

John Chow

Bill & Michelle Pescosolido

Jashin Howell

Rhonda Michele

Luke Lim

Carolina Millan

Chris Cobb

Guy Crawford

Ewen Chia

Kim Willis

Daegan Smith

Andrew Fox

Adeline Sugianto

Zack Carter

Junjun Li

Tim Atkinson

Terry Lamb

Paul O'Mahony

Matthew Dreier

David Gilks

Brian Price

Rob Paris

T.J. Rohleder

Georg Kerschhackl

Sue and Jerry Smart

Yannick van den Bos

Scott Smith

Aik Hoon Chan

Cynthia Nataline

Andrea Goodsaid

Nick Pratt

Chris & Susan Beesley

Michael Morin

Jeremy Miner

Ernest Lim

Saj P.

Chris Prefontaine

Robert Tepper

Vikas KumRai

Will Riley

Ken Faminoff

Alex Shelton

Deborah Robertson

Meidee Lim

Gavin Mountford

Norbert Orlewicz

To our MOBE Diamond members: A. Sugianto, A. Cheung and D. Halls, A. Goodsaid, A. Ashbolt, A. Chitty, A. Roshan, B. Abedi-Bedford, B. Barry, B. & M. Pescosolido, B. Smith, C. Millan, C. Fanner, C. Joly, C. Nguyen Vong, C. Shoemate, C. & S. Beesley, C. Cobb, C. Hines, CL Chooi, C. McDavid, D. Bundy, D. Betts Jr, D. Salkeld, D. Waters, D. Gilks, D. Reed, D. Myles, D. Jasa, D. Lofthouse, E. Lim, E. M. Ullrich, E. Ching Ang, E. Chia, F. Sgalbazzini, F. Goncalves, F. Hudacek, F. J. Torchia, G. Kerschhackl, G. Goff, G. Irby, G. Yang, G. Hedstrom, G. Gephart, H. Zainal, H. Abdelwali, I. Billingham, J. LePage, J. Brinkerhoff, J. Miller, J. Veverka, J. Corrigan, J. Ma, J. Teo, J. Marx, J. Hammond, J. Greiner, J. Sherrod, J. Chow, J. Collins, J. H. Davis, J. Cantu, J. Lindley, K. Louise, K. Ragland, K. Ponce Enrile, K. Eve, K. Maerki, K. Strickland, K. Willis, L. Crisp, L. Mannesse, L. Lafferty, L. V Leonard, L. Hell, Live By Design LLC, L. Tessari, L. Lim, M. Lundeberg, M. Allen, M. Prosser, M. Howley, M. Poynter, M. Lim, M. Bibat Ana, M. Passaglia,

M. Prochnik, M. Larin, M. Yong & W. Koh Koh, M. Lee, N. Pushparaj, N. Shen, N. Oktora, N. Pratt, N. Evashkevich, O. Haliv, P. Lynch, P. Gibat, P. Rodriguez, P. Schmitz, P. Beaudoin, R. Lynn, R. Manuel, R. Collier, S. Winn, R. Karim, R. Michele, R. Straight, R. Mackenroth, R. Lilja, R. Eckes, R. E. Patton, R. & R. Keenan, R. & R. Brock, R. H Herbert Jr, S. Olson, S. Oliver, S. & K. Smith, S. Hussyin, S. Ambrose, S. Turton, S. Wells, S. Ichikawa, T.J. Rohleder, T. Kulp, T. Lamb, T. Jin, T. Thomas, T. Donovan, V. Path, W. Hutchinson, Y. van den Bos and Y. Podzolkov.

To Raymond Aaron, who also happens to be a MOBE affiliate—we spoke about me writing my book on a Tuesday night before the weekend I wrote this; without that conversation and your extra little nudge to get it done, it would likely *still* not be done.

Our affiliates continue to promote our mission and purpose: to become the Number #1 educational resource for business owners and entrepreneurs in the world. MOBE is my life. You've heard entrepreneurs say that before, but I mean it; nearly everything I do I do for MOBE, though I have to admit I get some great perks along the way. I will continue to focus on making the MOBE high ticket affiliate program the most profitable program in the world. I guarantee you that. God willing, I'm not going anywhere.

Thank you all.

Foreword

By Raymond Aaron

Co-author of New York Times best-seller Chicken Soup for the Parent's Soul and author of the Canadian best-seller, Chicken Soup for the Canadian Soul

I first met Matt Lloyd when he asked me to speak at one of his international conferences in Phuket, Thailand. It's a long long way, but I accepted because I sensed something special.

I'd heard of Matt, of course. He was some kind of Internet marketing guru—but that's about all I knew at the time. When I arrived, I discovered that over 200 people had flown in from all over the world and paid over **$9,000** each to come hear him speak. Do the math, and you'll see that's one heck of an impressive amount. He was 28 years old at the time and he was the Founder of this impressive global enterprise MOBE.

Having hosted my own workshops for a third of a century, I know how hard it is to fill rooms, even at zero entrance fee. But to fill a large room at $9,000 per ticket, in far-away Thailand that everyone had to fly long haul to – wow, that's amazing!!

When we actually met and I shook his hand, there seemed to be nothing out of the ordinary about him, with his polite manner and soft Australian accent. He seemed like a regular guy. I almost wondered if I was meeting the wrong guy.

But later that day, when I saw him training on stage, I knew this was no ordinary man. Even though he'd made a lot of money, there was a very grounded humbleness about him; but at the same time, he was determined and positive. He wanted to lift others up. He genuinely cared about his clients and affiliates. He wanted to see them do well. He had a profound intensity about only one single purpose – his members must make a lot of money in affiliation with MOBE, no matter what!!

I assure you that when you apply the lessons of this book, you WILL create a completely new powerful and huge financial future for yourself.

How can I assure you that? Firstly I began using the ideas of this book myself and began earning at the rate of a new additional 6-figure annual income from my first month – without using my database at all. I wanted to see how ordinary people could do. It worked better than I could have ever expected.

Secondly, while still at that first MOBE seminar, I interviewed the highest income earners using the processes described in this book. They were all overjoyed. So I then interviewed the beginners just starting to earn, and they were overjoyed. I'd never met so many happy people. I ran around asking if people had any complaints. No one.

I had found a new home. I felt safe, cared for, and cherished. I was welcomed. I was amongst others who were already successful or eagerly on their way.

I now continue to use the powerful easy-to-implement ideas of this book, and my MOBE income just keeps rising. And I'm encouraging my tens of thousands of clients worldwide to grab this fascinating new opportunity.

You are holding your new financial future in your hand. Read the book and for sure check out the accompanying book website mentioned throughout the book.

Raymond Aaron
New York Times Bestselling Author
Happy MOBE Affiliate

Keeping Uncle Sam Happy

L et's get the disclaimers out of the way first: When I say "dollars" in this book, I'm talking about the U.S. kind. A lot of the success stories you'll soon hear about hail from the U.S. originally, even though many have since moved on to other parts of the world (usually tropical paradises!) because their newfound freedom has allowed it. And although we have success stories from all over the world, many are from the U.S., so we follow their regulatory rules.

I'm NOT going to promise you for absolute certain that the secrets I describe in this book will make you rich. Only you can do that, and it will come down to how hard you work, your tolerance of risk, and your audacity.

Not everyone who tries these methods makes money with them, just as not everyone who tries to lose weight through buying diet plans and exercise equipment gets results. Some people would rather stay home and stuff their faces with pizza rather than exercise and stick to the diet plan. Naturally, these lazy people skew the overall results.

The same is true for anything worthwhile, including my HTAM Method and the MOBE affiliate program that's based on it. While some people make no money at all, there are others like Darren Salkeld, whose team has been paid over *$8 million in cash* so far with MOBE. Throughout this book, and later on in Appendix IV, I'll be discussing my very best success stories, because I want you to see what's possible, and for you to get excited about what you can do!

But let me make it very clear that these are not average results.

The U.S. Federal Trade Commission (FTC) has many rules in place about what you can and can't say when presenting the results of a program. Even though my company and I aren't based in the USA, we like to abide by their laws. Some are a pain in the neck, but they're well-intentioned laws, implemented to protect people from being taken advantage of and misled—so I respect the FTC's reasons for having them.

When you see me talk about success stories in this book, they're all real people—ordinary folks I personally know who've generated hundreds of thousands or even millions of dollars. You can prove to yourself they're real by researching them on the Internet, if you like. But frankly, I'm hesitant to even talk too much about our very top affiliates and their results, since many people reading this may not even believe me. And truth be told, I don't want to insult your intelligence by assuming you think everyone who becomes an affiliate marketer and tries to make money online succeeds anyway. Like I've already said, the majority fail—just as the majority fail in any endeavor.

The majority of people who set New Year's resolutions don't keep them. The majority of people who start an exercise program have given up by the end of the first week. How many of those who buy exercise equipment from late-night infomercials starring toned models end up replicating their results? Very few. Why? Because they use the piece of equipment for less than a week, then fold it up and put it under their bed. It's difficult to stay dedicated to something that's difficult, even if it can be life-changing.

And I know for a fact that the majority of people who start reading this book won't even finish it. I fully expect that. But I'm not interested in talking to the majority. I'm interested in that minority of people who are at a point in their lives where they want and need to make a serious change. I'm talking to *you*. Yes, you.

So assume from now on that if I tell you about a success story, **that person's results are not even remotely typical**. I focus on them because I want to show you what's possible **if and only if** you put in the required time, energy, and work—and if you follow my training.

Will you be my next online millionaire success story?

Only you can answer that.

I'd like to be able to feature you in my next book. And maybe, if you really believe in and follow my instructions, I will.

Matt Lloyd speaking at an industry event in London, UK

Introduction

*L*imitless is a personal account of my journey from a small farm in Australia to the helm of a $100 million business that's poised to spring toward the billion-dollar mark. What you're about to discover in these pages has the power to change your life so far beyond recognition, financially speaking, that if I were to tell you by how much, you probably wouldn't even believe me.

In this book, you'll learn the secret to my success, and how YOU can use it to succeed in the New Economy.

What do I mean by "New Economy"?

I mean that, in the last two decades, that economy has changed forever. The days of working for a company for 35 years and retiring with a pension are over; it's more or less everyone for themselves. For most of us, this is scary; for others, it's exciting. It all depends on your viewpoint. You see, every major shift in our economy presents new opportunities to profit.

"You can have everything in life you want, if you will just help other people get what they want."

Zig Ziglar

Did you know that more millionaires were created during the Great Depression than at any other time in history, because it was an ideal time to start a new business? Real estate was cheap, and assets could be bought at fire-sale prices. For example: in the city of San Antonio, Texas, USA, the 12-story South Texas Building, once the tallest skyscraper in the city and worth multiple millions of dollars, was sold at auction for... $27,000! Even then, that was a ridiculously low price... and you can bet the new owners recouped the value many times over after the economy improved.

Today, the world's economy has shifted again, this time as a result of the Internet and globalization. It wasn't abrupt, but it's been inevitable. The Internet has seen its own series of shakeups as the social media-dominated "Web 2.0" has replaced the original static World Wide Web. Those who see this and can take advantage of the confusion can become millionaires just like those who saw opportunity in the Great Depression.

I first noticed this shift seven years ago, but I didn't know how to profit from it then. In fact, I spent the next two years working long hours (and spending everything I had) before I finally broke through and "cracked the code." That was the beginning of my HTAM Method that would go on to help generate over $100 million in the next five years. Since then, I've shared this idea with thousands of people all over the world, who have made a combined total of over $51 million with it. That includes affiliates, sales representatives, and others. And now, after five years, I'm finally ready to share it with you in this book.

The Internet Has Revolutionized How We Make Money

In order to understand the HTAM Method (pronounced H-TAM), you need to first understand that the Internet has changed *everything*, from how we communicate and how we shop, to how we get from Point A to Point B. Unsurprisingly, it's also changed how we make money:

- **You don't need a physical storefront anymore.** Amazon is the largest retailer in the world and they don't have a single store open to the public.

- **You don't need physical products anymore.** Google generates over $50 billion a year without them.

- **You don't need employees.** You can leverage systems, tools, and software to do most of the work for you.

- **You don't need to wait to get paid after fulfillment.** You can get paid up front before you deliver the product or service.

- **You don't need to be location-dependent.** You can work from anywhere in the world with an Internet connection (I run my online empire mostly from different Starbucks cafes).

This NEW kind of business model has extremely low overhead, and offers complete freedom and high returns. And while I'm not the only person in the world who has figured this out, as far as I know I am the only person in the world who has developed a method that allows anyone—regardless of age, experience, or financial background—to profit from it. This method can be applied by stay-at-home moms, retirees or soon-to-be retirees, college kids, and office "slaves" trying to escape their jobs. It's truly universal, because it doesn't matter where you come from or what your background is.

You don't need a college degree.

You don't need a lot of capital to invest.

You don't need to be "tech savvy" or great with computers.

Whether you're an engineer, a pastry chef, or a construction worker, you can apply the HTAM Method and make money with it. And the best part is, it's fast and it's scalable... which means that you can quickly double, triple, or even quadruple your income just by "turning it up." **There are no limits.** That's why I've called this book *Limitless.*

How to Live a Life Without Limits

The HTAM Method allows you to live a life without limits. Imagine...

- **Doing what you want when you want to do it.**

- **Living life by your own rules.**

- **Traveling all over the world.**

- **Buying nice things for yourself and your loved ones whenever the mood strikes—and not worrying about the cost.**

- **Creating income at will and having the time to enjoy it.**

When you apply this to your life, you'll be your own boss. You'll have freedom, security, and peace of mind. Money worries will be a thing of the past. In short, you'll spend more time doing the things you love with the people you love.

51 Million Reasons Why This Will Work for You

Regular people *just like* you have collectively received over $51 million in the last three years alone with this revolutionary method. A handful of people who have dedicated a lot of time and effort to it have made over $1 million each, while others happily bring in $3,000 to $10,000 per month with plenty of time left over to enjoy their new lifestyle. The HTAM Method is the basis for a revolutionary affiliate marketing program that I've shared with thousands of people around the world, many of whom have gone on to enjoy fantastic success. You'll read about many of them in this book, including John Chow from Canada, Paul Lynch from the U.K, Carolina Millan from Chile, and many others.

And in this book, you'll learn how YOU can use my HTAM Method to create a substantial income without the hassles of running a traditional business. *Limitless* will show you:

- **How to create a substantial income in your spare time working from home.** In fact, you can make more working part-time than most people make full-time!

- **Why you don't need to create or ship products, deal with customers, set up websites, hire staff, or start merchant accounts.** I reveal how this can all be Done For You.

- **How to apply the HTAM Method even if you have ZERO experience online and have never owned a business** (the genius is in how simple it is).

- **Specific examples of people from their teens to their 80s who have made money with this method.**

- **Why this is "borderless" and "ageless."** People in over 37 countries around the world have profited using the HTAM Method, including many Baby Boomers and retirees.

Here's What's Inside This Life-Changing Book

As you can see, *Limitless* isn't a thin eBook or glorified pamphlet. It's more than 200 pages of no-fluff content and real-world knowledge, including:

- **An Explanation of the HTAM Method**, including what it is, what it stands for, and how the MOBE affiliate program utilizes it.

- **Step-by-Step Blueprints** for mastering every aspect of the HTAM Method, from getting started to advanced scaling techniques that will allow you to hit 6+ figures per year.

- **Real-Life Case Studies** from my business (and others), so you can see how these ideas are applied in real situations.

- **Visual Guides** including charts and illustrations to help explain the core concepts of the HTAM Method and the MOBE system that utilizes it.

- **Mindset Shifts and Daily Habits of Successful People** that will help you grow in every aspect of your life (including business).

- **What to Do and What NOT to Do...** you'll learn how to avoid the mistakes I made (saving you time and money), and focus on what's been proven to work.

- **PLUS...** much, much more.

Throughout these pages, I'll introduce you to people who have used these ideas to set themselves up financially for *the rest of their lives*. As you read these stories, you're going to become very excited. At some point, you'll probably ask yourself that fateful question: *"If they can do it, then why can't I?"*

You can.

But it's going to take some hard work and dedication.

Commit to finishing this entire book. Don't let this be like countless other books that you may have started with good intentions, but ended up not reading and collecting dust. The skills and knowledge I teach here won't just soak into your brain by osmosis.

Seriously: Finish this book, and then actually *do* something. Make your dreams of financial freedom come true. Chose to create a life where you can go into a store and buy anything you want without having to worry about the price. Or travel anywhere in the world on the spur of the moment, knowing your business will still be making you money while you're gone.

My sincere hope is that you will read every page and change your financial life forever. I hope we'll meet some day, and you'll be able to tell me all about it.

CHAPTER ONE

Choosing The Right Business Model

As I type these words, it's Friday, 5:48 PM here at the Hilton Doubletree in Kuala Lumpur, Malaysia. I've booked the executive suite for three nights. Upon checking in, I informed the front desk that I didn't want the free Wi-Fi—in fact, I told them to make sure it would not work in my room, and to also not let any calls through. I don't want to be distracted, and I don't want to be disturbed. For the next 30 hours, I'll be focused on ONE task; writing these words and teaching you how you can make more in a month with your own online business than you currently make in a year. Potentially a lot more.

I've just crossed over the USD $100 million threshold in total sales of my products, services, and live events since starting MOBE. So far, I've handed out about $51 million of that as earnings to my sales representatives and affiliates. It may sound like I was able keep $49 million … and I wish that were true! But keep in mind I also have to pay for overhead expenses, taxes, and the salaries and benefits of a company that consists of 185 team members and growing, which adds up to small fortune. But I still got to keep some of it!

I'm 28 years old now, and I started my first online business at the age of 21. For seven years I've been doing this. The first two years, I was an abject failure. I made very little money; in fact, it took me nine full months before I generated my first dollar. And it wasn't for lack of trying; I worked long hours, and had spent my life savings on it (around $40,000).

The HTAM (High Ticket Affiliate Marketing) Method allows you to quickly create a substantial income as a new affiliate. To get a Free Bonus Video of Matt explaining "The Art & Science of HTAM" go to: www.fivefigureaffiliatemarketing.com

Then in late 2011, everything changed. I made $15,000 in the month of November of that year.

The next month, $45,000.

And then the next month, I grossed $81,000 in revenue. From there it's continued to go up and up. And up.

So I've been through it all. I know the very highs and very lows of trying to make money online; and I'm in the unique position of having enough personal experience (combined with the experience of coaching literally thousands of other people around the world) to know what I'm talking about.

That's me. Now let's talk about you.

If you picked up this book, you're obviously interested in the idea of generating money online from home. It could be to buy a bigger house, get out of debt, or quit your job and spend more time at home with your kids. Whatever your reason, you're interested in knowing more. Commit to finishing this entire book, and by the end, you'll have everything you need to be incredibly successful.

But before we move on, how much will you need to invest to start an online business like mine? USD $2,500 is the magic number. That's not so much in the great scheme of things.

In the chapters to come, I'll tell you why—and reveal how it works, starting with the most important element in Chapter 1 - Choosing the Right Business Model. In this chapter, you'll learn:

- **The Truth About Business** and why most traditional businesses models are flawed

- **What NOT To Do:** A personal example from my life of a business model you do NOT want to follow

- **What To Do:** Your solution to the "9 to 5" rat race

- **What You've Been Looking For:** *A business model that allows you personal and financial freedom*

Why Most Traditional Business Models Are Flawed

Choosing the right business model is one of the most important decisions you'll ever make, if not *the* most important. Having said that, I immediately want to point out that one of biggest time-wasters when starting a business is developing a formal business plan. Your ONLY plan when starting out should be to make your very first sales and bring in cash as soon as possible. It's as simple as that.

Now, before you do anything else, the first thing you need understand is that most traditional business models are *inherently flawed*. That's right. Most of what you've been told about "running your own business" is misguided. Let me give you an example from my own life that involves one of the oldest businesses in history - farming.

I grew up on a farm; and from a young age, I saw how hard running a business could be. Make no mistake: running a farm is indeed a business, possibly the *original* business, and every dollar counts.

My parent's farm is next to a small town of 15 people.

With my dad on the farm, age 8. To this day, my parents are still on the farm.

When I tell people I'm from a small town, they often assume I mean a few thousand people. But I actually mean about 15! That's right—the town I'm from is so small that everyone who lives there not only know the names of their neighbors, they know the names of their pets as well. It's a town called Lake Varley, in Western Australia; a place the British might call a village, or even a hamlet. The nearest "big town" (which we used to classify as over 200 people) is a good hour drive away. I'm not kidding.

I'm the youngest of four kids, and my parents are wheat and sheep farmers. To this day (they're now in their 60s) they still own that farm, and still work long hours.

Let's look at the business model of running a farm. This may not seem relevant at first glance, but trust me, it is.

With a farm, you spend a lot of money to put in a crop. You have to pay for machinery—tractors, seeders, and vehicles. You have to pay for fertilizer. You have to pay for staff. On a decent-sized farm, we're talking hundreds of thousands of dollars in costs to put that crop in. Where I'm from, that was usually done around March and April.

Once the crop is in the ground, the farmer spends another small fortune on chemicals to spray for weeds. If they don't, they're going to have a lousy yield and not much grain to harvest. So there goes several hundred thousand dollars *more* in expenses. As the year goes on, the farmer depends on one main thing,

In business, you don't want to be a price taker. You want to be a price maker.

and hopes like hell it gets delivered: good weather. It must rain at the right time of the year. It then must stop raining at another point in the year. It can't be too cold in the mornings. Growing up, I saw frosts wipe out entire crops my parents had grown, destroying just about everything.

If the timing is even slightly off with the weather, the farmer ends up with a poor crop. They get low-quality grain, they get a low yield, and they don't get paid much—if anything. And that's the worst part: they ONLY get paid at the

Harvest time at my parent's farm.

very end of all this, nearly an entire year later. So they have to front the huge sums of money necessary to plant and grow the crop; and if the other variables they can't control don't destroy everything, then they can get paid. Ironically, they don't even know how much they'll get paid until after they've harvested. They don't set the price; the market does. They produce a commodity exactly the same as what their neighbors produce, along with hundreds of thousands of other farms all over the world.

In business, you don't want to be a price *taker*. You want to be a price *maker*.

No matter how you look at this business model, it's a terrible one. It has ridiculously high overheads and capital expenditures, which you have to pay up front. You get paid only AFTER doing all the work, assuming the weather and 100 other variables don't destroy your crops. It's also labor intensive; many farmers work 18-hour days and more during busy seasons like seeding, harvest, and livestock birthing. And again, what you produce is a commodity; you can't charge more than your competitors, because what you produce is no different from what they produce... so there's very little room to add on margin at the point of sale. Add to all that the fact that the lifestyle doesn't suit most people, if only because you live in very isolated places away from civilization, and it's easy to see why suicide rates among farmers are the highest of any profession.

Farms are absolutely necessary for the rest of us to survive, but it's pretty clear that they are a poor choice for a business model.

The thing is, most businesses are similar to the Farm Model, in that you pour money into the business for a long time, sometimes years, before you see any money come back at all.

Think about it...

Restaurant owners spend hundreds of thousands of dollars before a single customer even sits down to eat. They have to find a space, build the restaurant, pay for expensive kitchen equipment, set up refrigerators and freezers, buy tables and chairs, hire staff (and train them), write a menu, establish relationships with vendors, and so on.

The "dream" of running your own business (whether it's a restaurant, salon, auto repair shop, clothing store, or something else) quickly turns into a nightmare when you realize how much it costs to get started and how much work it will take to recoup your investment and become profitable.

The sad truth is that 80% of small businesses fail within their first 18 months, costing their owners a lot of money and stress. Many end up right back where they started - working for someone else at an unfulfilling job because it provides a steady paycheck with a lot less risk.

But there's another way.

You CAN have your own business that gives you financial and personal freedom, and you don't have to risk hundreds of thousands of dollars to get there.

A Revolutionary NEW Model That Gives You Personal & Financial Freedom

This "good business model" is the complete opposite of just about all of the things I've listed about the Farm Model and other small businesses. In fact, the model itself is SO good that it can play a much larger role in your success than your own talents. Confession... many people who know about Internet marketing think that I must be a really smart guy and have some amazing talents. After all, I've done over $100 million in sales, right? Ha! If only they knew the truth! I *am* smart, but I'm not that smart. I *am* talented, but I'm not that talented.

Upon meeting me at one of my live training events (like the Titanium, Platinum, and Diamond Masterminds), most of my students are surprised to see that I'm just an ordinary guy. The fact that I chose the right business model has contributed to my success **far more** than any innate talent.

Here's what a good business model offers:

* **Low monthly overheads** that remain relatively fixed, even when sales rise fast and dramatically.

* **Ease of fulfillment**, even at rapidly increasing levels.

* **Payment up front**, before delivering the product. I don't lift a finger unless someone pays me first. If they want to consult with me, they pay me $5,000 an hour and must buy a minimum of five hours at a time. After I get the money, then I do the work. Note how this is the complete opposite of some business models, like running a farm.

* **Minimal legal risk and potential for getting sued.**

* **A business that isn't location-dependent.** You can operate it from anywhere in the world: your home, Starbucks, your hotel room, or a beach that has Wi-Fi.

* **Customers who aren't location-dependent.** As long as they have a credit card and an interest in what you're selling, they can buy your product and receive it from anywhere in the world.

* **You don't need to keep coming up with new product ideas**, month after month.

* **You don't need to keep creating new marketing campaigns**, month after month.

* **You don't need to hire staff** unless you really want to; and if you do, they can work for you from anywhere in the world with you being able to track their productivity.

* **You don't need to have merchant accounts** to process orders.

* **You don't have to deal with customer support.**

Does all this sound like a wonderful business model? Does it sound too good to be true? Well, it is true—and it's called affiliate marketing.

In the next chapter, I will explain affiliate marketing in more detail.

CHAPTER TWO

An Introduction to Affiliate Marketing

P lain and simple, affiliate marketing is the ultimate business model of all time. I'm not exaggerating for effect here. I did it for many years (before launching my own affiliate program and teaching others how to do it). An affiliate's cost of fulfillment is outrageously low. If an affiliate promotes a digital training course, their cost to deliver someone their login details is virtually nothing. They get to keep a percentage of the profit, which can be incredibly high. Of course, there is some overhead, like the costs involved in placing ads. But compared to traditional business models (like running a brick and mortar business, or even a farm) those costs are a drop in the bucket.

In this chapter, you'll learn:

- **What Is Affiliate Marketing?** You'll learn exactly what affiliate marketing is and why it's a legitimate business.

- **The Basics of Affiliate Marketing** and the first things you need to do to get started.

- **The Affiliate Link** - Where affiliate marketing starts.

- **How to Get Fast Results By Focusing on ONE Traffic Method**

- **The Curse of Low Ticket Affiliate Marketing**

- **The Joy of High Ticket Affiliate Marketing** (and why this should be your focus)

◆ **The 3 Levels of Affiliate Marketing**

Let's get started…

What Is Affiliate Marketing?

Because they've suffered at the hands of MLM or other, similar business models, many people mistakenly think of online affiliate marketing as somehow shady. It's not. Most companies like mine are not out to fleece the affiliates; they need their affiliates to make money and to scale their businesses. One or a few people can only do so much; thousands can build a marketing empire.

And there's certainly nothing shady about getting paid a commission for connecting a company with a new customer. Many businesses operate this way. If you've ever bought a car, you've dealt with a commissioned salesman. The same is true for furniture salesmen, real estate agents, or any other individual who brings a customer into a company for a finder's fee or a part of the income earned. It's a practice that's many hundreds of years old; it's proven, time-tested, and still common today. If you're a good salesperson, it's a far better way to make money than a normal nine-to-five job that pays an hourly wage or salary. In fact, your income is effectively independent of the number of hours you work. You can make $10,000 in an hour on one day, nothing for the next, then $5,000 the third—and you've still beaten the pants off most jobs.

The only difference with affiliate marketing is that you're not a salesman. In fact, you don't have to do any of the selling if you don't want - the website you're placing ads for can do all of the selling for you.

Explained another way, here's how affiliate marketing works…

Let's say I develop a training product for business owners who want to learn how to create their first website and start collecting leads. It's priced at $1,500. They're happy to pay it, because if they implement the strategies I teach in this training product, they'll be able to generate thousands of leads for their business which could be worth hundreds of thousands of dollars. $1,500 is a no-brainer.

So I have this product, and I have a website that explains all the benefits of the product and how someone can buy it. But I have no website visitors. And with no one to see my website, I can't make a single sale.

That's where you come in. You become an affiliate for my business by joining my affiliate program, and your role is simple; to bring a potential customer to my website. That's it! Once they are on my website, I can then sell him or her my course. If they buy it, I agree to split the $1,500 with you. After all, without you, I wouldn't have made the sale in the first place. Only seems fair, right?

So how much of the $1,500 do you get paid?

Different affiliate programs will pay different amounts to those who close the sale. Some pay 10% commissions; others will pay up to 50%. A rare few will (like me) pay even more. It all depends on what their cost of fulfillment is, and how greedy or generous they are. If they are too greedy and pay out tiny commissions, affiliates won't promote them. Why should they? There are plenty of other businesses that will compensate them better. But, if they're too generous, their margins will be terrible and they may not be in business long... and that's not good if you're an affiliate waiting to get paid!

Now... let's come back to your role; getting people to someone else's website. How do you do this? First, you acquire an affiliate link from your new affiliate partner, one that's unique to you. Then you place ads on other online venues: Facebook, search engines, forums, chat boards, other websites, etc. You may not know this, but a huge percentage of the ads you click on online aren't actually placed by the business owners selling the products. They're placed by affiliates, people who place ads and get clicks (traffic) in order to earn commissions.

You could go on Facebook right now, post a link to someone else's website, and have someone click that link in the next 30 minutes. That is what 'driving traffic' is; sending people to a website. The only difference between you and an affiliate marketer is that you're not getting paid to send traffic (yet!). So, just how much traffic do you need to send to a website in order to make your first commission?

That depends mostly on two things: the people who make up your traffic, and how good the website is at making an irresistible offer that gets people to buy.

Now, you may be wondering why these business owners who have websites don't just place their own ads, so they can generate their own traffic without having to pay affiliates a commission. Well actually, *most do*. But the Internet is so enormously large and vast, that they choose to get additional traffic from affiliates because they can't reach it all on their own.

In this chapter, I'll teach you the basics of affiliate marketing and how to get started. Later on, I'll invite you to join my own affiliate program (the same one that has paid out over $51 million to people like you all around the world).

The First Thing You Need To Do To Get Started

Although affiliate marketing is by far the easiest way to earn money online, there's still a learning curve. Luckily, it doesn't have to be a steep one. It's entirely possible to be earning money within a few hours from now if you take action. There are a lot of shortcuts to making your first commissions, and programs like the MOBE high ticket affiliate program are built to help you take advantage of them. We call these 'turnkey' programs, because all you have to do is put in a key (your affiliate link) and turn it (drive traffic) to start making money. Just about everything else is done for you. The creation of the products, websites, customer service, processing of payments, and much more. Affiliate marketing is the 'lazy persons' way to making money online because someone else has already done most of the work.

Even if you don't know much about computers or navigating around the Internet, you can get started. When I started, I knew nothing. I hired a computer science student for about $12/hour to come to my home office for a few hours each week, and show me the basics. They showed me how to buy a website name (or what's called a 'domain name,' like www.mobe.com), how to get hosting, how to set up an email autoresponder so I could follow up with my leads, and how to start generating traffic.

You see, the company I was with before I started MOBE didn't offer much for its affiliates. No websites. No lead-capture pages. No coaching, No assistance at all.

The first thing you should do when you start any new business, is focus on bringing in cash.

They expected you to hit the ground running, knowing how to do it all yourself. I didn't hit the ground running. You might say I went *splat.* But I got up and started pushing forward, and I wasn't afraid to find help even when I could barely afford it. It took some time, sure—but there wasn't as much to learn as I thought, since there were already tools available for me to build my business with.

The first thing you should do when you start any new business, is focus on bringing in cash.

Sounds obvious right? Of course you should focus on getting some customers and making some cash. But so many people waste time creating logos, setting up their business cards, going out and buying stationary, or doing other 'busy things' that don't directly bring in the critical ingredient you need to grow; cash. Don't spend days watching videos or reading books and blogs without implementing the things you've learned. All that falls under the category of *'getting ready to get ready.'* My rule of thumb is that for every hour you spend learning, go spend 3 hours *doing.* Learn as you go, and don't be afraid to make mistakes. And if you feel like there's too many things to learn, then focus on the things that will bring in money right now. Learning to place ads and generate traffic is a lot more important than learning how to design a logo or improve your technology. Until you make money, you can't do much else to grow your business.

HTAM CASE STUDY

Nick Pratt Escapes Corporate World and Makes $116,450 with the MOBE High Ticket Affiliate Program

My name is Nick Pratt. I'm 28 years old and from Nottingham, UK. To date, I've made $116,450 with the MOBE high ticket affiliate program! My best day so far was $8,800 in one day, which was an incredible feeling. Unlike some other programs, MOBE actually works and allowed to me escape my corporate job.

After finishing university at the age of 21, I went straight into the corporate world. However, it wasn't long before I was burned out and disillusioned with working as an employee. So at age 23, I looked for something else – I wanted the freedom of running my own business. This led me to Internet marketing, affiliate marketing, and other home business opportunities. Unfortunately I went through a lot of programs before MOBE that didn't work as advertised.

But I didn't give up. I kept searching and eventually found MOBE, which was a breath of fresh air. I knew that "high ticket" was the way to go and I saw MOBE as paving the way in that area. I am grateful to have found MOBE, which has changed my life.

Nick Pratt (Diamond Member)

Remember, in affiliate marketing your job is to **find a great offer and put people in front of it.** That's all it boils down to. You become an affiliate for that offer (or website), get an affiliate link, and get the right people to click it. When they buy, you get paid your commission.

The Affiliate Link: Where Affiliate Marketing Starts

Your affiliate link might look something like this: **www.mobetrack.com/ ifs/5kla553**. That's could be a standard MOBE affiliate link for a course we sell, like 'Internet Funnel System,' one of our bestsellers at $49 (which pays a $44.10 commission to you).

Look at the elements of that link. That "mobetrack" indicates it is a tracking link for MOBE. The "ifs" is short for Internet Funnel System, so we know what to credit you for. And the alphanumeric designator, in this case 5kla553, could be your affiliate ID number.

Every time someone clicks that link, the click is tracked as having come from your affiliate link through a combination of cookies (little pieces of code), and the IP address and email address of the person doing the clicking.

Affiliate links are all unique. If you become an affiliate for MOBE and decide to promote one of our products, like Traffic Masters Academy or the Titanium Mastermind, you'll get unique links for each product. Every time someone clicks that link, a cookie is left on the browser of the person doing the clicking. A cookie is a little piece of code that tracks where you've gone and makes it easier for your computer to reopen that website when you go back. It's a very accurate way of tracking referrals so that affiliates can get paid a commission on any sales they referred.

NOTE: If all this sounds like mumbo-jumbo to you, don't worry. You don't need to know how it works, you just need to know that it's very accurate and ensures that you get paid your commission on all people you refer to the website you're promoting.

First Touch vs. Last Touch Affiliate Tracking: What's The Difference?

Most affiliate programs are last-touch, because it's the fairest kind. With a last-touch affiliate program, whichever affiliate places the ad that brings in the sale gets the commission.

Good affiliate tracking software (like the one we use in MOBE) is very accurate. Even if someone buys from our website three months after clicking on your affiliate link, you'll still get credit for the sale (unless they clicked someone else's affiliate link after yours). With first touch, someone else might have gotten a click from a lead one year ago, but not produced a sale. Then you come along, spending your time and money to get that person to click again and see the offer, and they buy. You got the person to buy, but you don't get paid (unknown to you), because that person clicked someone else's link a long time ago. Most people would agree that's not fair at all, but that's how 'first touch' works. So we make sure we stick with last-touch every step of the way. You deserve to get credit on the sales you made.

How To Get Fast Results By Focusing On ONE Traffic Method

Once you have an affiliate link or links, your ONLY goal is to get people to click that link and look at the offer.

Seriously—forget everything else. If you drive enough of the right people to a high-converting offer, a small percentage *will* buy, which will result in you getting paid commissions. Until you become good at driving traffic, nothing else matters. So don't get distracted by all the shiny objects out there; focus 100% on getting traffic and making those first commissions.

I have some very successful affiliates—one of whom has made over 4 million dollars in the MOBE high ticket affiliate program—who have made the majority of their money through being very good at just one method of traffic.

After you pick the right offer to promote—preferably one that pays high-ticket commissions like MOBE—then focus like a laser beam on driving traffic (people) to it. To do this, you'll have to buy ads. Forget about free traffic, at least for now; it's way too slow. Buy as much paid traffic as you can afford each day, generate commissions, and then use your profits to buy more. Focus on only ONE type of traffic and become an expert at it. It doesn't matter if you choose solo ads, Facebook pay-per-click, Google AdWords, or some other advertising method; they all work. I even have affiliates who stick strictly to newspaper ads (*yes, you can generate a lot of traffic by advertising offline!*). Amazingly, they've made hundreds of thousands of dollars that way.

Don't waste time and dilute your efforts by trying too many traffic methods. Pick one, and become good at it. The more targeted prospects you can get to click your affiliate link, the more money you'll make.

Remember this advice; make sure you choose the right place to advertise your affiliate links; you wouldn't advertise pork products in an Orthodox Jewish religious online forum, no matter how much traffic it gets!

The target market and the offer you're promoting must be a match.

Whenever someone clicks your link, they get sent to the offer page / website, and then the business you're promoting takes it from there. Every couple of weeks, depending on which affiliate program you promote, you'll get paid.

Now I'll let you in on a little secret; most companies you promote only pay you a one-time commission when you send them a customer. Then, they follow up and make additional offers to that customer for more expensive products, and this is where the real money is made. Often they're able to make 10 to 100 X more money from those follow-up sales (what we call 'the back end'), than from the first one you got paid on. And you don't see a penny of it.

The MOBE high ticket affiliate program is different though. If you send MOBE a customer, we pay you commissions on ALL the back end sales we make to that customer. Most of our affiliates make over 80% of their money from these back-end sales, and they don't have to lift a finger. We do all the additional sales for them. The policy at MOBE is that you get paid commissions on the customers you send us *for life*. Anytime someone you've introduced to us buys something new, you earn a commission—no matter how much it is or how long afterward it happens. It's not uncommon for an affiliate of MOBE who initially made a $44.10 commission on a $49 sale to later pick up a $1,250 commission, and right up to a $10,000 commission. All from the same customer, and even if those sales are made more than 1 year later!

Later, if you want to develop your own list (your own collection of leads you can market to again and again), you can send people to a lead-capture page where they're asked to put in their email address by filling out a form (more on this later). They give you their contact details and permission to email them. On average, for every 3 people you get to your lead capture page, one person will 'opt in.' Sometimes more. Once they're on your list, they're your subscribers and you have permission to send them emails (which you should do on a regular basis) and make other offers. A good, responsive list can make you **large** sums of money every time you hit 'send.'

More on this later, but first let's discuss the price points of the products you'll be promoting.

The Curse of Low-Ticket Affiliate Marketing

Most companies offer relatively low commissions for their products, because the products are lower priced. Most will be under a couple hundred bucks. Commissions of 40% or less are typical. So for example, you might promote a book for $50 and only get a $15 commission, or a video course that sells for $300, and get a commission of just $80. Rarely will they pay you on the back-end. Most companies are just too greedy and lazy to offer you a percentage of the extra money they make to the customers you sent them. This is one reason why even successful online affiliate marketers sometimes give up; without those back-end commissions, they can't make decent money promoting low priced products.

Here's a quick question for you: if your goal was to make $10,000 each month, would you rather do it by selling 1,000 products each month which paid out a $10 commission each, or, would you rather sell 10 products that paid you a $1,000 commission each?

Both will get you to $10,000 each month. But one is much easier than the other.

High-Ticket Affiliate Marketing (The HTAM Method Explained)

I never liked the idea of low-ticket affiliate marketing. It seemed like too much work for too little money. So I invented a category I call "High Ticket Affiliate Marketing" or HTAM (pronounced H-TAM).

Companies that use this business model have actually been around for a while, but hardly any affiliates know about them. For most, you literally have to be invited into their private affiliate program, or stumble across them accidentally. That's how I got started in affiliate marketing: I stumbled across one of these companies while doing an innocent Google search, looking for ways to make a lot more money than I was making from my lawn-mowing business at the time. That company had 3 main products, priced at $1,755, $9,000, and $15,000.

On each sale, you made $1,000, $5,000, and $9,000 respectively. But you had to literally make the sales yourself by calling back your leads, referring them to a sales webinar held each night, then following up. That company didn't have a phone sales team like MOBE does, which does the sales calls instead of the affiliates.

I'd never seen anything like this business, but it intrigued me. I ended up investing my entire life savings into it (and whatever I could borrow from friends and family). Over the next couple of years I got to see all the flaws with the way that company was run, and it was the ultimate training program for me to one day start my own company.

HTAM CASE STUDY

Baby Boomer Carol Douthitt from Chesterton, Indiana Gets Excited about Her Retirement Income Options When She Makes $48,445.50 with MOBE in Her First Three Months

As a member of the Baby Boomer generation, approaching retirement without enough savings can be scary enough. But the thought of slinging burgers or wearing a blue smock and working a cash register all day was far from the way I had envisioned spending my Golden Years. I knew there had to be a Better Way.

I had been researching several online businesses and was watching the progress of MOBE for over a year before I decided to join them in March 2015 as a Platinum Affiliate.

I was really impressed with the owner, Matt Lloyd, and the commitment he had to growing his business while giving his affiliates the training and tools they needed to be successful with their businesses.

In my first 3 months I made over $48,445.50 in commissions! I also attended their event in Las Vegas, spent a week in the Dominican Republic, and I'm scheduled to travel to a gorgeous resort in Fiji next month!

Whoever thought retirement could be this good!

Carol Douthitt (Platinum Member)

But the one thing I always liked about their model was that they focused on much higher-ticket items than most other affiliate companies out there. **And from that they could afford to pay much larger commissions.**

Let me expand on that last point since it's so important...

The High-Ticket Affiliate Marketing model pays out much larger commissions to new affiliates (like you), and allows you to create a full-time income working part-time from home.

The MOBE affiliate program is a HTAM (High-Ticket Affiliate Marketing) system that shares BIG commissions with you on

The High-Ticket Affiliate Marketing model pays out much larger commissions to new affiliates (like you), and allows you to create a full-time income working part-time from home.

high-ticket back end sales. Not only that... all the work to generate those high-ticket sales is Done For You (no other company does this quite like we do). In fact, you can make commissions of up to $10,000 per sale if one of your leads buys one of our high-ticket conferences on the backend!

How many of those $10,000 commissions would you need to make each month in order to have a good month?

My point exactly.

Later on in this book - after I've taught you how to get traffic - I'll explain this method in more detail and tell you how to get started with the MOBE high ticket affiliate program. But first, let's get the right foundations in place.

The Three Levels of Affiliate Marketing

At my live training events (including the Titanium, Platinum, and Diamond Masterminds), I teach that there are three different 'levels' that affiliate marketers may go through while building their businesses:

Level 1: Send cold traffic.

Level 2: Send warm traffic.

Level 3: Create your own products and sales funnels, and selling them instead of (or alongside) the products you promote as an affiliate.

All new affiliates (including you) should start out at Level 1. Starting out at Level 2 or 3 means you'll be trying to learn too many new skills at one time, instead of focusing on one. As you advance through these stages, your potential profits increase, although you can still make a fortune at Level 1. I myself am in the Third Stage. I have my own products, services, and live events that we sell through all the different sales funnels we use. I employ dozens of staff, have an enormous international operation, and get paid very well to run this operation. But I work non-stop. Even though most people want my money, they wouldn't want my life. Don't feel sorry for me, though; I'm doing what I love, and working 14-hour days, seven days a week is fun to me.

Getting to the Third Stage isn't for everyone. If your goal is to make six figures a year, then you don't need to get to the third stage. In fact, it's entirely possible to get there with Level 1. In the next chapter, I'll teach you how to prepare yourself to master Level 1.

CHAPTER THREE

How To Set Yourself Up For Success Before Spending Your First Dollar On Ads

W hen you watch a star athlete in action, whether it's boxing, basketball, football, tennis, or golf, they make winning seem effortless. That's because they've put in the work, practice, and training to get to a very high level. They've also done their mental "homework," which means they *know* they're going to win before they even play.

Spending money on traffic is no different.

You need to understand the rules of the game before you start wildly buying traffic and placing ads. If you put some time in to learn these fundamentals, you'll have a much higher chance of being successful (and making more money). Fortunately, this doesn't take years for affiliate marketers (like it does for athletes). If you apply yourself, you can learn these fundamentals in a matter of days and start seeing results almost immediately.

In this chapter, you'll learn:

* **How to Find The Right Niche** and the advantages of the "business training" niche

* **Why You Need to Learn The Language of Your Market**

* **The Value of Targeted Traffic**

When you join my High Ticket Affiliate Marketing Program at
www.fivefigureaffiliatemarketing.com you get your own personal coach to walk you through a
simple, 21 step training program on how to make your first big commission online.

- **How to Use The Right "Bait" To Attract Your Ideal Customer**

- **How Understanding Prospects & The Buying Spectrum Will Exponentially Increase Your Profits:** Ignore this at your own risk…

- **How To Get Inside the Mind of Your Prospects**, and target hyper-responsive buyers

Let's get started…

How To Find The Right Niche

Finding your niche and target market ALWAYS comes first. Don't promote a product and then try to find a target audience for it. Choose your audience first. In this section, I'll talk about my favorite niche (business training).

Why did I choose the business training niche?

First, I love business. I grew up around business (my parents business was the farm), and I loved the idea of helping others start a business, make a lot of money, and change their lives. Ever since I started my first business on the side of the road at the age of 10, selling potatoes to passersby, I've been hooked.

The other reason I chose to sell training to existing and aspiring business owners was ROI—Return on Investment. By demonstrating the ROI of the training you are selling to your prospect, you can sell very expensive programs that pay huge commissions. I have programs that pay our affiliates up to $18,000 per sale (and I'm working on new ones that will pay even more)

Now, you might be wondering, *"Who in the world would spend that kind of money on a program?!"* But remember… just because a program sounds expensive to you doesn't mean it sounds expensive to others. Recently, I had a client pay $10,000 for a five-day coaching program, just a few months after he'd paid $56,000 for another four of my programs. I later found out he had his own tax accounting business that was netting him over $700,000 a year. To someone running a business of that level, high-dollar programs that teach them how to make even more money don't sound expensive at all; they sound like a good investment.

Also, I don't just sell to these types of business owners. I'm one of them. I have no problem spending tens of thousands of dollars to get one-on-one coaching from experts. I rationalize the decision by thinking, *"If I implement this advice, how much extra profit can I make this year?"* It's nearly always a lot more than the investment, so I spend the money. In fact, last year, I spent over $200,000 on consulting and seminars that would help me take my company to the next level. Imagine how much money you would have made if you'd been the affiliate placing the ads online that got me to buy those programs!

When I got started, I decided I'd rather sell expensive programs to a few customers paying over $50,000 per year each, than cheap programs to tens of thousands of customers paying just $10 each. The first option has a lot less headaches than the other. And now, you face the same choice. You can promote one of my MOBE programs that pays $1,000 per sale, and make your first $100,000 online with just 100 customers... Or, you can try to make $100,000 promoting courses with $10 commissions - which means you'd need 10,000 customers!

Granted, it *is* slightly harder to find customers who'll pay higher prices than those who won't. But it's not *proportionately* harder. Most people willing to spend several hundred dollars on a course will just as easily spend several *thousand* dollars if the product you promote is valuable enough, and is pre-sented in an irresistible way.

I love selling training programs to business owners. I have a passion for it and think it's a "dream niche" for anyone getting started in affiliate marketing. But if you prefer something else, then you'll need to do some research.

Look for a niche where people are in urgent need or want of products and are almost rabid in their willingness to spend money for new things. Ironically, buying most solutions only causes people in the truly active niches to want to buy even more. You'll want to enter a large, busy niche, where there's already

When you join my High Ticket Affiliate Marketing Program at
www.fivefigureaffiliatemarketing.com you get your own personal coach to walk you through a
simple, 21 step training program on how to make your first big commission online.

lots of businesses selling to the prospects. Don't look at competition as a bad thing; it's a good sign there's people making money.

Browse the magazine section on Amazon.com or in a large bookstore, and see what niches have the most titles represented. Or just go to Clickbank.com and look at the different categories under the 'Marketplace' in their menu. Some are pretty tame and slow; some are full of products that have high 'gravity scores,' which indicate lots of affiliates are making sales promoting them.

The people within the most profitable niches want or need something to ease their pain, whether it's emotional, psychological, financial, or physical. The pain is what drives them to go searching online for answers, where you will have strategically placed your ads right in front of them. And the pain is what helps motivate them to take action now and buy, rather than procrastinate.

Remember: finding your niche and target market ALWAYS comes first. Don't promote or create a product and then try to find a target audience for it. Choose your audience first.

Why You Need to Learn the Language of Your Market

Once you've chosen your niche, you need to learn its specialized language. In every niche, there are "insider terms." Think of your favorite hobby. There are terms used in that hobby that an outsider wouldn't understand. Do you know what a 'proof' is, or a DCAM69? How about an Indian head or Morgan CC? An avid coin collector knows those terms. Anyone who's going online and typing those terms into Google is clearly an insider—otherwise, they wouldn't know the words to search for.

It's the same with the online marketing niche. If you and I started talking to a stranger using specialized online marketing terms, we'd get blank stares. If we mentioned "targeted traffic," they might think we were talking about cars on a road who were in severe danger of being shot at by a sniper! And once we started talking in acronyms, like PPC (pay per click) and CPC (cost per click), we'd have lost them completely. Whatever niche you're going to promote affiliate offers in, make sure you learn the language of that market so when you're writing ads, you can get the right people clicking your ads (and exclude all the wrong people).

Here are another couple of other terms we often use in the traffic business: "qualified traffic" and "self-qualifying." The people closer to the end of the buying spectrum are more qualified than those at the beginning, and in fact have self-qualified themselves to an extent by getting this far. They're also going to be the most expensive to target, because everyone wants them. But it's worth it; even if you have to pay two or three times the money to reach these people, that's often a much better idea than trying to target the unqualified masses and hoping one of them will buy. Think of it this way: if you're a hunter, would you rather shoot at a herd of deer with a slingshot, or would you rather go hunting with a rifle with a precision scope, and be able to hit exactly what you're aiming for? If you're an angler, would you go fishing for sunfish with a shark hook, or would you pick the smallest hooks you could find, hooks that actually fit their mouths?

The best analogy I ever heard about this was from a guy called Howie Jacobson, when he said something along the lines of, *"Untargeted marketing is like trying to shoot a mosquito with a shotgun."* So spend some time learning the language of your market, so you can lure those closest to the buying end of the spectrum to your products.

How to Use the Right "Bait" To Attract Your Ideal Customer

Marketing guru Dan Kennedy talks about knowing "who you're going after," and offering the right 'bait' to attract the right buyer. He says if you're hunting elk and you use cheese as your bait, you're going to attract a certain animal alright—*but it's not going to be the one you want.* You have to know your perfect customer so well, that you can guess what they're thinking as if you're standing in their shoes, looking out of their eyes.

When you join my High Ticket Affiliate Marketing Program at
www.fivefigureaffiliatemarketing.com you get your own personal coach to walk you through a
simple, 21 step training program on how to make your first big commission online.

As an example, when you're marketing MOBE programs you're targeting business owners. The type of business owner and what they need help with depends upon the product, service, or event you're promoting. If it's a course on outsourcing, you'll be targeting business owners who are ready to hire. They're already making sales, but struggling to keep up with demand while doing all the work themselves. You wouldn't target a business owner who just started last week; that person is going to be a lot more focused on getting their first few sales than bringing on new staff.

How Understanding The Buying Spectrum Will Exponentially Increase Your Profits

Let's talk about the process a prospect goes through when making the decision to buy. This is important to know and understand, because any time you're getting traffic, that traffic will be made up of people at all locations on the buying spectrum. Marketing to one end will make you a lot of money, while marketing to the other end can make you broke.

Here's an example I usually share with students during our live training seminars, including the Titanium Mastermind.

Think back to the last time you bought a new car. Did you just wake up one morning and say, *"I'm going to go buy a new car today!"?* Did you then go right down to the local car dealer, say, *"I want that one!"* and pull out your credit card? I doubt it. That's not how you buy a car. Instead, there was a longer, more drawn-out process involved.

Here's what likely happened: At some point, you began to notice your existing car was getting a little on the old side. The air conditioning wasn't reliable as it used to be. The engine was making funny noises. The paint was beginning to fade. You thought, *At some point, I'm going to need to get a new car.* But you were too preoccupied with whatever else was going on in your life at that point to give it any more thought.

A few days later, the thought entered your mind again, perhaps triggered by your latest discovery of what was getting worn out. This time, the thought lingered for a little longer. You took it a little more seriously. And then you remembered that new car commercial you'd seen on TV recently... but again, life got in the way, so your attention moved elsewhere.

The next day, you started thinking again about getting the new car (notice how the frequency of the thought is now increasing). You went online and started looking at what was available: the different makes and models, the different prices, and the locations of several nearby car dealers you could visit that weekend. You asked yourself, *"Should I buy secondhand? Should I buy new? What car can I see myself driving? How much do I have in the bank to put towards this?"*

These thoughts, along with your actions of actually searching online, are legitimate **buying signals** to marketers like me. No longer do you just have a vague desire; now you're seriously thinking about getting a new car.

So that weekend, you went down and test drove a few new cars. You really liked three of them, made by three different manufacturers. You liked the smell of the leather—that classic new-car smell—and how much better they handled than your current clunker. The price of each was much higher than you wanted to pay, but you were already thinking of ways you can finance it. You went home that night to think about which one you wanted. And again, you went online to do just a little more research on each car.

The Million Dollar Question...

So ask yourself this: If you're an affiliate marketer placing ads online for one of these three different types of cars, at which end of the spectrum do you want the people clicking your ads to be?

Realize a solution   **Desperate for a solution**
is needed.   **and ready to buy.**

HTAM CASE STUDY

Nancy Showalter – Retired American Woman Builds Nest Egg & Supports Lifestyle Abroad With Commissions From MOBE

My name is Nancy Showalter and I'm a retired woman from Springfield, Illinois, U.S.A. To date, I've made $19,759 with the MOBE high ticket affiliate program and my biggest day so far was $8,800 in one day!

Before retiring, I was the manager of inbound call center and worked for non-profits for many years with low pay. In 2008, I resigned and we moved to Ecuador. But because my non-profit career had paid very little and had no retirement benefits, we did not have any real retirement nest egg or income. We loved Ecuador and South America. We loved the people and our beautiful home in the serene mountains. But we worried we wouldn't be able to afford living here without another source of income.

That's when I discovered MOBE. I immediately saw the opportunity to generate the income we needed to become financially free and live wherever we wanted.

When I earned $8,800 in one day, it was amazing. And it was even more amazing to realize that I had actually earned $11,961.50 in my first month of business! It was a fabulous start. I attended the Titanium Mastermind in November and received a trophy from Matt for Excellence in Achievement. The mastermind and the Leverage Summit prior to it were awesome events. All the leaders and high-earners were more than willing to help and share their strategies. And the resort was incredible. As a newbie, these events made a huge difference in my business.

Nancy Showalter (Platinum Member)

Do you want them to be at the earliest stage, where they've thought once or twice about a new car? Or do you want them right at the final stage, well educated on what options are available, and much closer to wanting to spend their money?

Of course it's the latter. When you place ads as an affiliate, your goal is to put those ads right in front of the prospects in your niche at the final stages of the research process, where they're doing their serious due diligence, educated on the options available, and about to make a buying decision.

Yet all the time, I see new affiliate marketers trying to buy clicks from the masses who are right at the start of the buying process (or worse, have no interest in whatever is being promoted). It's no wonder they don't make a commission.

Many new affiliates are scared of paying higher prices for traffic to people the end of the spectrum. This group of people is much more finite than the outer rings of less targeted traffic...

...but this targeted traffic source is much more likely to result in you getting sales, so it's well worth it.

How To Get Inside The Mind Of Your Prospects & Target Hyper-Responsive Buyers

If you've already been in affiliate marketing for some time, consistently generating traffic but not making sales, then there's an obvious reason: you're targeting the wrong group of people. It's like you're selling cars, and yet you're getting clicks from people who are perfectly happy with their existing cars and have no desire to get a new one. You may be wondering, *"How do I find these people who are at the end of the buying spectrum, ready to spend money?"* The first and most obvious answer is to put yourself in their shoes and ask, *"Where would they most likely go?"* or *"How would someone in that position behave?"*

When you join my High Ticket Affiliate Marketing Program at
www.fivefigureaffiliatemarketing.com you get your own personal coach to walk you through a
simple, 21 step training program on how to make your first big commission online.

People's behavior online can tell you a lot about who they are and how close they are to buying.

People usually go through the same process when buying online. They begin as an uneducated prospect, doing a very broad-based search on their options. Let's take the example of someone like me back in late 2008, who wants to learn how to make money online, but has no clue how to do it. One of the first places they'll go to is a search engine like Google, Yahoo, or YouTube. Sitting in front of that empty search box, they begin. What would that person type in?

I want you to start thinking about these kind of things, and getting into the minds of your prospect. Would this person type in a search phrase like "affiliate marketing?" Not yet; this person doesn't even know what affiliate marketing is yet. Instead, they'd start with a very generalized search like, "Make money online." Every month, this three word phrase gets typed in on google. com hundreds of thousands of times.

If you're in the business of showing people how to make money online, and you can get your website ranked in the natural search results on this page, it can be worth a lot of money. It's also one of the most competitive search terms in the online moneymaking niche. In December 2015, Google recommended you bid at least $2.15 per Google AdWords click if you wanted to use "make money online" as your keywords. That's just *clicks;* there's no guarantee anyone will sign up for your lead capture page, much less buy what you're selling. Furthermore, other people will be getting their versions of the same AdWords online. So right away, our prospect is presented with a bunch of options they can click on. They're usually going to click on more than just one.

And they start to learn. They learn that yes, it is possible to make money online, and there are several methods of doing it. One of the methods they keep seeing is "affiliate marketing." They think, *Hmmm, sounds interesting—let me learn more about that.* So they go search again, this time for "affiliate marketing." A whole new set of results comes up—completely different to the first. This phrase is searched for "only" 74,000 times per month, much less than "make money online," but then again we'd expect that, since it's a more specific phrase that fewer people would know about.

So the newbie starts clicking the different websites shown, and learning about how affiliate marketing works—about the business model, and about these things called 'cookies' that track sales back to the marketing efforts of specific affiliate partners. They probably subscribe to a few marketing lists and are soon getting emails from many different marketers—people like you and me, who spend time and money to get their marketing in front of these people.

They start to read about different places where you can become an affiliate and start earning commissions. One of these is a site called Clickbank.com: a competitor to MOBE, with a lots of products to promote, but much, much smaller commissions. They go and check out that website, and start to learn about how it all works. So when they decide they want some training, they go back to Google, and type in "Affiliate marketing Clickbank tips."

Again, they get a completely new set of search results. They find all kinds of different websites—and they find all kinds of different courses that teach how to market with Clickbank. They're now a little overwhelmed about which ones to buy. They're open to the idea of spending money to get the right training, but want to make sure it's the right program.

So they go back to Google and search for "clickbank affiliate marketing training." Once more, a whole new set of results comes up. Turns out this phrase is searched for only about 10 times each month. They start reading about Clickbank guru trainers, and all the different products they can buy.

Now, let's say there's a course on how to do well with affiliate marketing promoting products on Clickbank offered by MOBE, and you're an affiliate for MOBE. You want to promote (place ads) for this product so you can earn some commissions. I'll give you 2 choices on where you can advertise.

1) On the "make money online" search results; and 2) On the 'clickbank affiliate marketing training' search results. Both are about the same price per click. Which do you choose?

The bullseye area with the most targeted prospects is also the smallest in size. But that's where the hyper-responsive buyers are, so that's where you're going to make the most sales.

The answer is pretty obvious, right? You want to get clicks from the second source. There will be a lot less clicks as the latter is searched for much less - but the clicks will be more targeted. They will result in a lot more sales (and a lot more commissions for you). For every 100 clicks you get from each traffic source, you could get *10 times* more sales from the second than you will from the first. It's not that the 100 people clicking from the "make money online" traffic don't have money or aren't willing to buy. It's just that they're not at the stage of being ready to buy a course on Clickbank affiliate marketing.

The further along the buying process you go, the fewer people there are. It's just like that archery target. The bullseye area with the most targeted prospects is also the smallest in size. But that's where the hyper-responsive buyers are, so that's where you're going to make the most sales. If you're targeting people in those outer rings, then it's still possible to make sales, but you have a much harder job facing you. Someone who doesn't even know what affiliate marketing is probably won't want to buy a course on Clickbank affiliate marketing. You'd need to do a lot of telling and selling before they would part with their money.

Personally, I much prefer to shoot fish in a barrel—ideally with the water drained out!

CHAPTER FOUR

How To Send Cold Traffic & Generate Commissions

I n Chapter 2, I told you there were three levels of affiliate marketing, and in Chapter 3, I showed you how to get ready for Level 1 - Sending Cold Traffic.

At this level, you won't have your own website, offer, or sales funnel. All you'll have is an affiliate link for someone else's offer. Your immediate task is to get the right people to click your ads, and have enough people clicking each day to actually make sales. If you only have one or two clicks coming in daily, you're not going to make much money. But if you can get dozens or more clicks coming in each day, you can start generating commissions.

The reason it's called "cold traffic" is because the people doing the clicking usually aren't going to the website you're promoting with a "warm" endorsement of any kind. In fact, they don't even know you exist. Affiliates usually start out at this first stage, and this is where I recommend you start out. In this chapter, you'll get a "crash course" in cold traffic, including:

* **Why You Should Start With Cold Traffic**

* **How to Generate Large Quantities of Quality Clicks With ONE Traffic Source**

* **How to Avoid Getting Ripped Off When Buying Traffic**

* **Targeted Vs. Non-Targeted Traffic**

- **Free Traffic Vs. Paid Traffic** (and why paid traffic is the lifeblood of your business)

- **How To Scale Paid Traffic With A Concept Called "Starve The Ponies, Feed The Stallions"**

- **PLUS... Lessons on Performance-Based Media and Fixed Cost Media, and Winning Ads That You Can "Swipe and Deploy"**

Why You Should Start With "Cold" Traffic

Why do I recommend you start with cold traffic?

Because you should only learn one skill at a time.

You don't need to learn how to get traffic and master copywriting, email marketing, creating websites, and webinar selling all at the same time. The first skill you need to learn is how to consistently drive traffic each day. To do this, you need to focus on ONE traffic method first. So pick your traffic method, whether it's PPC, solo ads, banner ads, or whatever — none is inherently better than the others — and hone your skills to the point where you can consistently send 50+ clicks per day to an offer.

Until you're consistently generating traffic to your affiliate links, don't even look at getting involved with the two more advanced levels.

There's a common misperception that you can't make big money in this business until you become famous as a "guru" and build your own brand. That's wrong. One of our MOBE affiliates is among the highest earning of all time—he's made **over $4 million in commissions** with us in the last two years. If I told you his name, you wouldn't even know who he is. He keeps a very low profile; he doesn't want to be a famous Internet marketing guru. He prefers to quietly make millions of dollars a year and live in his beach house in California.

Often people try and skip the traffic part, and start learning about how to build their own blogs, how to create their own products, how to send out emails to a list. It's ridiculous! They're setting themselves up to fail. Because until you, as a new affiliate marketer, can consistently generate traffic (clicks) to a link each and every day, and put lots of people in front of an offer, you've got no hope of getting paid. I've said this numerous times already, but it's worth re-emphasizing yet again:

The first thing you need to learn how to do as an affiliate marketer is generate traffic. You are in the business of generating both quantity and quality of clicks to an offer.

Reread that three times, please. It's that important.

How To Generate Large Quantities of Quality Clicks

First, you're in the business of getting a decent *quantity* of clicks to an offer. If you're only getting two people a day in front of the offer you're promoting, you're not going to make many commissions. Depending on where you're getting your clicks from, maybe only 10 out of 100 people you get to a website are going to be truly interested, and maybe only two of those 10 will be open to buying. So if you're only getting a couple of clicks a day, that means it could take you 50 days to get your first commission. You're not going to get any real momentum behind you at that pace.

On the other hand, if you can generate 50 clicks a day (which is only about two people clicking your ads every hour), then you have a real chance of making some sales… provided, of course, those are *quality* clicks. This is the most important part. Remember, behind every click is a real person, with thoughts, feelings, and desires. Just because you have a lot of clicks coming in to an offer doesn't mean the people doing the clicking are going to buy. If they are the wrong people for the offer, you're not going to get sales.

Here's an example—a little ridiculous—but it makes the point. Let's say you're promoting someone's knitting product: "How to Knit Better Quilts." Obviously, it's for people who like knitting. I don't know about you, but in my mind I think of a little old lady sitting in front of her fireplace, knitting all day. So an affiliate marketer comes along and wants to start promoting this course so he can earn some commissions. The course sells for $30, and pays a $10 commission. He finds a website that's getting 100,000 visitors a month, and has some really cheap banner ad space. Bingo! He buys the ad space from the websites owner for $100, sends them his affiliate link and banner ad (you can get banner ads made for cheap on fiverr.com). The banner ad is really 'loud' - it's got big, red flashing letters that say, "CLICK HERE for a Surprise!!!" Soon he's getting 200 clicks a day—a good quantity of clicks, right?

But after a month, and over 6,000 clicks, he hasn't made a single sale. Why? What could possibly be wrong? It's at this point that most new affiliate marketers might give up and say that affiliate marketing doesn't work.

What I didn't tell you, was that this website getting 100,000 visitors a month is for image conscious men and is all about lifting weights, getting 'buff' and 'ripped,' and what protein powders they recommend. It's about as far away from a 'knitting' audience as you could get!

Hundreds of these guys are clicking the 'loud' banner ad each day, but immediately upon seeing a website featuring a grandma asking, *"Would you like to learn how to knit better quilts?"* they're thinking, *"what is this?????"* before exiting 2 seconds later.

My point is this; even if you can get hundreds of clicks a day, it doesn't mean you'll automatically get sales. There has to be the right offer-to-audience match. And this is exactly what I'm talking about when I refer to the *quality* of clicks.

The quality of a click comes down to *who's* doing the clicking, and whether they're a good fit for the offer. For a knitting product offer, those 200 clicks / day were poor quality clicks for that offer. If the offer was about getting 6 pack abs, then those clicks could be high quality clicks. It all depends on the offer-to-audience match.

Here's another example: if I'm promoting a book like the one you're reading right now, I would want clicks only from people who have some or all of these characteristics:

* **They're interested in learning how to make money online right now**, and ideally they want to make large sums of it.

* **They're open to starting their own business**, as opposed to spending the rest of their lives working for someone else.

* **They understand there's an investment required to start a business**; they're not looking for something for nothing.

* **They don't have the mindset that all "make money" programs on the Internet are scams.** They're not. Most of the people who spread those rumors are failed affiliate marketers who never placed even one ad.

If they meet all those requirements, I'm very open to spending money to place ads in front of them that they'll click, so I can get them in front of my offer.

With MOBE, I can teach you how to do all that. In fact, one of our primary programs, "Traffic Masters Academy" is all about that, and some of our live events teach advanced traffic methods, including the Titanium Mastermind. These trainings can have you placing traffic and making money quickly— possibly in a matter of in days.

I know I keep saying this, but I'll say it again; there are literally *thousands* of ways to generate traffic to an offer, but you only need to get good at one. Focus on just one, until you absolutely master it. One good traffic method can make you a fortune. As I write this, I have at least five affiliates who've made over $1 million in commissions with our affiliate program. I have over 38 people who've made over $100,000 in commissions, and many, many more approaching their first $100,000 fast. Just about every single one of them has one main traffic method they've used to get their results—and they're all very different from each other.

- Diamond members Bill and Michelle Pescosolido have made over $800,000 in the last two years getting the majority of their leads from Facebook Pay Per Click (PPC).

- Darren Salkeld (Diamond member of course) has made over $8,000,000 in commissions by finding buyers from the CPA (Cost Per Action) networks.

- Diamond member Shaqir Hussyin, with close to $2.7 million in commissions, has generated the majority of his sales from marketing to other people's email lists, using solo ads.

- Another guy does product launches on different affiliate networks, where other affiliate marketers promote his stuff, and then goes and promotes MOBE programs to all the buyers. He's also closing in on $3 million.

- One of our stars places banner ads on popular Internet marketing forums.

- One of them gets a lot of leads from Skype. Somehow they add the right people to their contact lists.

- One uses a plain Facebook page to attract people.

- Two of them (another husband-wife team) from Sydney, Australia don't even know how to place ads online—they say it's too technical for them! Instead, they place ads in their local newspaper and in magazines, and they've made hundreds of thousands of dollars doing so.

- A guy from India who used to make $700 a month working at Walmart has made over $92,000 in his first year with the MOBE high ticket affiliate program, largely from promoting a "15-minute call" with himself on Facebook and Skype, where he then sells a $49 MOBE product (and MOBE takes over from there).

By the way, just to be up front with you: I don't know the exact amounts these affiliates have spent on their traffic to generate those kinds of commissions. Some of them may spend $1 for every $10 they generate in commissions. Others may spend a lot more. But obviously, their efforts have been profitable, or they wouldn't keep promoting. At no point do I say (or have I ever said) to our affiliates that they could generate commissions without investing time, money, or more likely both into building their business. This is hard work. I'll never pretend otherwise.

The point I'm making with all this is that you only need to get good at one traffic method to make good money online.

And then here's a question I always get from affiliates: *"Matt, what's the best traffic method for getting sales?"* I hate to burst their bubble, but there is no best method. How well a particular method works largely depends on who is executing that method in the first place, and who they're reaching with it. Remember our knitting example? Just because our affiliate did not make any commissions from all those clicks he got from the banner ad, it doesn't mean that banner advertising doesn't work. It *does*; you just need to be reaching the right audience, at the right price.

> *Ultimately, how well you do with your traffic all depends on who's doing the clicking.*

Facing the painful truth... Ultimately, how well you do with your traffic all depends on who's doing the clicking. If it's your ideal customer avatar, someone who's looking for the solution you offer and is ready to buy, then those clicks are worth paying a premium for. It's less about the traffic method you use to reach a prospect, and more about making sure the people you're reaching are the right prospects. When people say a particular traffic source doesn't work, the truth is they just weren't targeting the right people. If you're promoting a weight-loss product, and use a solo ad to target people who don't want to lose weight and won't buy what you're promoting, it would be ridiculous to conclude that solo ads don't work. But people do that every day.

The other thing they do, when capturing leads themselves and then handling the follow-up (at Level 2), is blame the traffic source for a lack of sales. More often than not, it's their lack of follow-up / conversion skills that's responsible for the low sales. As long as you're buying from legitimate traffic sources, rarely is there such a thing as "bad traffic," as in a group of people who just don't buy. Most of the time, it's an issue of the wrong offer for that traffic, and bad follow-up. When you consider that traffic is made up of people, and that all people regularly spend money on something, and have needs and desires... then it makes no sense to blame the traffic for non-buying behavior.

Targeted vs. Non-Targeted Traffic

In my office, behind my desk, I have a high-powered compound bow. From time to time, I stand up, pick up that bow, nock an arrow on the string, and fire it at about 250 feet per second into a foam target on the other side of the room. The bow is there for target practice, and to shoot when I need a break... and also for finance staff who make mistakes when handling my money!

(Kidding)

Each time I shoot that bow, I aim for the bullseye in the center of the target. Archery has been a hobby of mine for years. The bullseye is the smallest and hardest part of the target to hit. It requires the most precision. The outer rings have ever-increasing surface areas the farther out you go, so they're easier to hit—but are worth fewer points. The same general concept applies to targeting prospects when you place ads online.

The general masses of people you see walking down a busy street during lunch hour in your city are what we'd call "untargeted prospects." There are a lot of them, and they're really easy to hit with your marketing. Go stand on a street corner and distribute 1,000 flyers, and you'll hit 1,000 of them. But from untargeted traffic, it's very hard to get sales for most offers. You may get lucky every once in a while and have 1 person out of the 1000 get your flyer and say *"this is just what I've been looking for!"* - but that's rare and requires a bit of luck. You don't want to build a business based on luck.

I define 'targeted traffic' as traffic made up of people who think often about the problem your product solves, or the benefits that it delivers. Let's say you're promoting a weight-loss course for young men. It's marketed as a "get six-pack abs" course. The ideal prospect you're targeting should already have an interest in getting six-pack abs—and should have bought similar "six-pack ab" courses before. That last part is really important. The best clue to see if someone is willing to buy your program is whether they've bought similar programs in the past. You may think that they'd be less interested in buying, but that's not true at all. Unless the product they bought was a one-time fix, which is rare, people who buy one product will usually continue to buy similar products.

Think of the lady who owns 200 pairs of shoes, or the guy who's fanatical about golf and owns four sets of clubs. A buyer is a buyer is a buyer, just as a non-buyer is a non-buyer is a non-buyer. We want to market to people who have demonstrated in the past that they're willing to pull out their credit cards and spend money.

Always go for the easy sales first. Go for the low hanging fruit.

Also... with whatever offer you're promoting, there's going to be some kind of benefit. Let's say your offer is promoting a product designed to stop nose-bleeds. When will our target audience go looking for our solution? When the blood is flowing.

In this business, it's best to sell the *cure*, rather than selling prevention. No one wants to buy prevention; people don't think that far ahead. Instead, we want to market to people who have an urgent need to find a solution *now*, so they can avoid some consequence. The more urgent the need is, and the bigger the consequence, the more likely they'll buy from us now. And the more willing they are to pay higher prices.

Chances are, you bought this book because you were looking for a way to make more money, and to do it from home on your own hours. Chances are there are consequences if you don't make this change—like unhappiness, debt, not seeing enough of your family, etc. So you felt compelled to take action immediately, and not put it off for later. In your marketing, you want to target people who are looking for your solution and ready to take action, just like you were when you bought this book.

Then again, there are people who might not need something right away, but are fascinated by a particular category of products. Consider the "make money online" niche. There must be hundreds of thousands of courses out there that claim to teach you the secrets to online riches. Most of them are garbage, and made by people who've never had any major success online - but business opportunity seekers (i.e., junkies) will keep buying these courses forever. What most of them are really buying is **hope**. Each time they pull out their credit card and buy, they're buying the *feeling* of hope that this product is going to be their savior—and a lot of them mistake the good feelings that come with buying with actually making progress.

I used to be a business opportunity (biz opp) seeker. If you're one now, let me give you some advice a mentor once gave me: biz-opp seekers don't make much money in this industry. Strategic entrepreneurs who think like real business owners (and who sell to the biz-opp seekers) make the money. I didn't start making sales myself until I made that mental transition of thinking strategically, rather than opportunistically. It wasn't until I stopped looking for the magic bullet that was going to make me millions for nothing in return, and began to focus on building a real business, that I made progress.

Free Traffic vs. Paid Traffic (And Why Paid Traffic Is The Lifeblood Of Your Business)

One of the greatest lies ever perpetuated by online marketers selling traffic training products is that there is "free traffic." There's not. All traffic has a cost. Some traffic costs a lot more than others, but there's always a price to pay, and you always end up paying it. Even if there's no financial outlay, but you spend hours of your time implementing the strategy, that's a cost because your time has value.

Most people starting their new affiliate marketing businesses want to make commissions, but don't want to spend any money to make them. They've never spent money on "clicks" before. It seems like a bad idea to spend money on something they can't even see, that may or may not result in a sale. So they decide to 'play it safe' and focus on the so-called free traffic methods - things like Search Engine Optimization (SEO), getting videos ranked on YouTube, or getting articles ranked for high-traffic keywords. For example, someone selling a course on how to make money online might try writing an article about it, and getting it ranked for the highly competitive search phrase "make money online"—which gets searched for about 135,000 times a month on Google alone. Go try this for yourself... and after 6 months of trying, come tell me how well you did.

I think by that stage, we'll both agree that it's not exactly free.

Same with video marketing. To make videos that actually get a lot of views, you need to make *good* videos. They always need to be highly informative and/or entertaining. Good videos can be made fast—but they still take time to make.

Remember: no matter what you spend your time on, there's always an opportunity cost associated with it (the highest paid alternative use of your time). If you spend three hours trying to write a great blog post with just the right keyword density so it gets ranked, you have to consider that those three hours could have been spent working in some job that paid you cash and benefits. So the blog wasn't free; it cost you whatever you could have made trading your time for money. Depending on the job you do or once did, that could be $50 or it could be $300. I'd rather use my time for higher-leverage activities than writing blog posts.

That said, one of our top affiliates, Diamond member John Chow (who's made over $2.2 million), gets a lot of traffic from his blog and using SEO. Is it free, though? No. He's been building that blog for well over a decade. He must have thousands of posts by now, and he's invested a lot of time into getting good at SEO. That's not to take anything away from him, and I'm not saying SEO doesn't work. Clearly it does. I'm just saying the concept of it and other traffic methods being "free" *is not true.*

While building a business, one of the most important questions you must ask yourself is, "How much is my time worth?"

If you have two hours a day to work on your affiliate marketing business and your goal is to make $100,000 in commissions, that means your time needs to be worth about $137 an hour. Any time spent on activities that pay less will make it very hard to reach your goal. So it doesn't make sense to do anything you can outsource for $10 an hour just to try to save some money. Even worse, if you're trying to learn SEO and don't know what you're doing, you can literally spend months going in the wrong direction, doing it all wrong, without making any progress. And why? Because you wanted to save a little money.

You can't save your way to making a fortune in business.

There's such a thing as being too attached to your money at the beginning. I was guilty of it myself. I'd spend hours each day trying to write articles that I hoped would get ranked in the search engines, so I could get those "free leads." I also bought a bunch of courses that promised to show me how to generate endless free leads. To this day, I've yet to find one that actually delivers. So when you're starting out, use paid traffic. As someone once said to me, *"don't step over dollars to pick up pennies."*

One of the best things about paid traffic is that it's scalable. In late 2011, I literally doubled my monthly revenue growth. I went from doing close to $7,000 to doing $15,000. Two months later, I went to $45,000. The next month, $81,000. People often ask, *"How'd you do it, Matt?"* Easy! I just reinvested proportionately larger amounts of money back into my traffic campaigns and resisted the urge to go and blow it all on fancy cars and new clothes, which is what a lot of newly rich marketers do. I do recommend that you take some money off the table when you're scaling fast—especially if you're at a later stage in your life. But I started in my early 20s, so I knew I'd have plenty of time to make the money back if things went south.

Paid traffic also gives you near-instant feedback. Rather than waiting weeks or months to see if your marketing is successful, you can find out within days, even hours. For example, did you know that the name of one of the bestselling books ever, *The 4-Hour Workweek*, was chosen based on feedback from running Google AdWords? The author, Tim Ferriss, ran some ads with different book titles to see which would get the highest CTRs (Click-Through Rates).

Instead of just choosing a name for his bestseller, he let the results of a paid traffic campaign tell him the best title—fast.

If you want to run traffic to an offer as an affiliate, with paid traffic (something like Facebook PPC), it's possible to get 100 people in front of a sales offer by this time tomorrow. It's very difficult to do that with something like SEO.

While building a business, one of the most important questions you must ask yourself is, "How much is my time worth?"

Also - just about all the biggest businesses are built on paid advertising. I can't name any company that does over $10 million per year and sells information courses online that has reached that size using "free traffic." So the next time you hear someone telling you they know the secrets to making millions of dollars online from free traffic, my advice is to ignore them. They're either misinformed or lying to you.

Now, despite what I've just told you, you're still going to be tempted to go the "free traffic" route. Most people are, and it's mainly because they're terrified to lose money. They're afraid they'll spend money placing an ad, and then have nothing come back in return. No commissions. And again, it'll happen to you. I can say with absolute certainty that occasionally, you're going to go spend money (or time, which is the same thing) placing ads, and get no results.

Just like any toddler who wants to learn to walk will take quite a few tumbles, you will spend money on clicks that don't make you any commissions. That's how you learn. And the good thing about it is, when your money is at stake, it will force you to learn very quickly. When pain is involved, lessons get learned much faster.

If you want to get good at boxing, you're going to take some punches along the way...

Years ago, I decided I wanted to start boxing. So I found a local gym, got a coach, and he started teaching me footwork and how to punch. After a week I got impatient, and told him I didn't need to practice the fundamentals anymore; I already knew them. I was ready to start sparring. So he put me in the ring with someone else at the club—a girl. *"Are you serious?"* I thought about my coach... and then looked at my opponent as if to say, *"Don't worry, I'll go easy on you."*

The bell rang, and 30 seconds later she'd bloodied my nose. Turns out she'd been boxing for years, and even though I *thought* I knew the fundamentals, like "keep your hands up," I didn't. When there were real consequences for getting it wrong (like pain) I started to learn my lessons really quick!

Trying to learn how to generate traffic by reading and watching courses, yet never risking any of your money, is like trying to learn to box without actually sparring. If you want to learn properly, you have to get in the game and place some ads. Go spend a few dollars—it doesn't have to be much. But spend something. If you're only comfortable with $5 / day, that's fine. Of the people who don't make money with affiliate marketing, a huge percentage never even go and place their first paid traffic ad.

How To Scale With A Strategy Called "Starve The Ponies, Feed The Stallions"

Like I said earlier, one of the best things about paid traffic is it's scalable. Paid traffic allowed me to go from $7,000/mo to $81,000/mo within the same year (2011)! And as you begin to scale your affiliate marketing business, you're going to have multiple ads out there at the same time. Even though you should only be using one main traffic method to start, you should have numerous ads targeting different keywords, or groups of people, because not all of them will be profitable. That's all part of the business, which is why you need to watch your numbers at all times. And this is where the concept of "starve the ponies, and feed the stallions" comes into play.

I learned this from fellow marketer Ryan Deiss—and I've never forgotten the lesson. What it means is that when you have ads that aren't making money, you stop running them right away and redeploy your funds into the ads that are profitable, and scale them up. Let's say you're promoting a $49 MOBE course, and that with our marketing process, your average lifetime value of each customer is $200. In other words, you can afford to spend up to $200 to get one, though you'll want to spend as little as possible to maximize your margins.

After choosing a traffic method and placing your first ad, you start getting clicks. Then you place more ads. Within a couple days you might have five ads running. Depending on what you're comfortable with, after two weeks your results might look like this:

Ad Number	Number of New Customers	Total Ad Spend	Average Cost to Acquire a Customer	Commission Generated
1	0	$200	$200	$0
2	4	$200	$50	$800
3	0	$200	$200	$0
4	0	$200	$200	$0
5	2	$200	$100	$400
Total	**6**	**$1,000**	**$166.70**	**$1,200**

At the end of this period, you've spent $1,000 on clicks and you've grossed $1,200, so you've made yourself a $200 profit. That's a 20% return—pretty good, right?

Warren Buffet became a multi-billionaire by averaging slightly over 20% annual returns year in, year out, and reinvesting the profits, so 20% is nothing to be scoffed at.

If you were to do the exact same thing next month, and continue to spend $1,000 each cycle, plus the $200 of profit, you could earn yourself a decent living. You might go from investing $1,000 per month, to $1,200, $1,400, $1,800, $2,200, $2,400, and so on, slowly building your monthly profits.

Of course, this assumes the traffic sources continue to attract the same rate of buyers, which doesn't always happen in the real world. And that's the danger of making a profit (*yes, there's a dangerous side to it*). The profits from some traffic sources can cover up the losses from others. It happens all the time, and the only one way to avoid it is to track your numbers.

Every one of your affiliate links should have a tracking link, so you can see exactly which ads are making money, and which ones are losing money. All good affiliate programs like MOBE's let you create tracking links quickly (in minutes). As long as you're tracking everything, you'll be able to implement "starve the ponies, feed the stallions."

Your stallions in the above example are Ad 2 and Ad 5. Ad 2 gave you a 300% ROI, while Ad 5 gave you a 100% profit. The ponies are Ad 1, Ad 3, and Ad 4, which brought in nothing. Results are rarely this simple or clear-cut; this is just an example.

The point is, you'd immediately stop spending money on the "pony" traffic sources; you'd starve them. Then you'd put all of your money for the next period into Ad 2 (Ad 5 made us a great return, so the moment Ad 2 stops making above 100% ROI, we'd immediately start putting money back into Ad 5 again).

Here's what the next month might look like if the traffic source continued to pay off:

Ad Number	Number of New Customers	Total Ad Spend	Average Cost to Acquire a Customer	Commission Generated
2	20	$1,000	$50	$4,000
Profit				**$3,000**

See the difference?

Because you were tracking your sales, and reallocating your ad spending to the traffic sources that offered the highest ROI, you're now making a $3,000 profit, not just a $200 profit. For the same amount of money you invested the first time, you're making $2,800 more—14 times what you would have made were you not tracking!

I hope you're getting this, because I'm giving you the secret to scaling your affiliate marketing business FAST—so fast, in fact, that it's possible one year from now to have so completely transformed your financial life that it's unrecognizable. This is EXACTLY what happened to me between the months of September 2011 and September 2012, when I made my first million dollars online. I went from having an empty bank account to having more money than I knew what to do with.

But it gets better. After making your $3,000 profit, let's assume you were able to control your urge to immediately spend it—like I was—and instead, you decided to invest it. Here's what the next month would look like, assuming you invested your normal $1,000 *plus* your $3,000 in profits:

Ad Number	Number of New Customers	Total Ad Spend	Average Cost to Acquire a Customer	Commission Generated
2	80	$4,000	$50	$16,000
Profit				**$12,000**

And then suppose you did the same thing the next month, investing your normal $1,000 plus the $12,000 in profit:

Ad Number	Number of New Customers	Total Ad Spend	Average Cost to Acquire a Customer	Commission Generated
2	260	$13,000	$50	$52,000
Profit				**$39,000**

HTAM CASE STUDY

Swedish Rock Star Discovers MOBE
and Makes $100,000/Year

My name is Rob Paris and I'm from Vaxjo Sweden. To date, I've earned about $200,000 through the MOBE high ticket affiliate program. My best day so far was $28,000! Everyone told me this wasn't possible, but I KNEW it would work and was determined.

I've always been a dreamer and something of an outcast. I was born in Sweden, one of the richest and most expensive countries in the world. Instead of going to university, I followed my dream and played music. I achieved a level of celebrity in Sweden, but not enough to pay the bills. I ended up working dead end jobs to survive, including delivering packages and being on the road 7 to 12 hours a day. Then I discovered Internet Marketing and decided to change my life. I worked hard for about a year, but didn't see any results. I was depressed and almost quit.

Then I found MOBE and its high-ticket affiliate marketing program. And even though I didn't know anyone in the industry, had no money, and lacked functional English, I made it work. I learned important lessons from my MOBE coach and kept at it. Soon after, I qualified for MOBE Motors, where MOBE paid for my dream car. (Details about MOBE Motors program at: www.mobemotors.com) 6 months in, I broke the $100,000/year mark and to date I've made over $200,000 through the MOBE high ticket affiliate program.

Rob Paris (Diamond Member)

If you kept this up for 12 months, total profit would end up being a very large number indeed. I'm not going to show you what it would be, because I don't want to mislead you into thinking this kind of growth can continue indefinitely from the same traffic source. It can't. At some point, diminishing returns will set in, and you'll need to find other traffic sources and boost them while letting your existing stallions rest; or, if necessary, cutting them loose altogether if they become ponies.

But is it possible to literally double your revenue from one month to the next in the world of affiliate marketing? Yes. It does happen—I've had it happen to me many times, and so have my top affiliates. The trick to maintaining rapid growth is to stay on top of your numbers, and as soon as certain traffic sources stop being profitable, cut them off and reallocate funds to ones that are profitable. The marketer who doesn't track and reallocate funds into the most profitable traffic sources is like the person living on top of a gold mine without even knowing it.

Now you're probably wondering... how much should you spend before you decide an ad is no longer profitable? What about those ponies? At what point do you decide you've found a pony, and cut them loose? That depends on what an average customer is worth to you, or the average Lifetime Value of a customer. If, as in the example above, a customer is worth $200 to your business, then paying anything up to $200 to test a traffic source is reasonable. So if you've spent $100 on a traffic source and haven't got a sale, it's still too early to make the decision on whether it's profitable or not. Even at $150, it's still too early—although the closer you get to your limit, the more closely you should be watching.

Once you exceed $200 in expenses, you have to make a judgment call. If you're a brand-new affiliate marketer and don't have a lot of experience with buying traffic, you're better off playing it safe. If you have some experience under your belt, you might keep going with a traffic campaign, even when it doesn't seem profitable.

Personally, I'm fine with paying more for my customers than my competitors, because I'll continue to make more offers to them as I create new programs that add value to their lives. I know that over the long term, some of them will buy. It doesn't take many of those customers buying a $10,000 program to suddenly make an ad buy highly profitable. And keep in mind that I've sold programs worth right up to $120,000 (my current record) to a single customer before.

With those price points, even the scrawniest pony can become a mighty stallion!

Many of my MOBE affiliates know this, and that's why they can spend more money promoting our products than just about any other affiliate program out there. Any customer they send us, we track for life. It's not uncommon for a MOBE affiliate to make a $1,000 commission (or much more) on a customer they referred to us two years ago.

Performance-Based Media Explained

Performance-based media is another kind of traffic where you pay every time someone takes a specific action (e.g., clicks an ad).

Are you trying to appeal to everyone? Of course not. If you place some Facebook PPC ads, the last thing you want is everyone on Facebook clicking your ad. For one thing, there are over 1.4 billion Facebook users—so that's going to get real expensive, real quick. And even if you could get them all to click, you wouldn't want them all. You only want the people who are most likely to buy. Because you have a limited ad budget, you want to screen out the people who are least likely to buy. Your goal here is to get the most qualified responses only.

Think of it this way: if you were handing out flyers at a busy intersection for a new luxury shoe store, and each flyer cost $5 to produce, your goal wouldn't be to give everyone a flyer. Do that, and you'll soon have wasted thousands of dollars. Instead, you want to hand out as many of those flyers as you can to qualified prospects. You might stand near a competing luxury shoe store, and each time someone came out of that store after browsing, you could hand them a flyer, since they clearly have some interest. You'd keep doing this until the competitor caught on to what you were doing and told you to go away!

Pretend for a moment you're a MOBE affiliate, and, you're promoting one of our outsourcing courses to business owners. It's priced at $497. The course is specifically aimed at business owners who are about to hire their first few staff, but are struggling with doing it. So you want to appeal to:

* **Business owners already running operations with more than one staff member**

* **Business owners with plans to hire more employees soon**

* **Business owners struggling with hiring right now**

* **Business owners willing to invest in training**

The people you definitely don't want are those unwilling to pay for training or invest in themselves, and people who don't have a business. So the ad might look something like this:

FEEL LIKE YOU'RE DOING THE WORK OF FIVE PEOPLE IN YOUR BUSINESS?

This four-week training program, available for a special price in this limited-time offer, will show you how and why that's NOT what your business was meant to be like. Call today!

Notice how the ad specifically calls out business owners? Non-business owners are unlikely to click this ad and will cost you money. The text makes it very clear that this is a paid training course, who it's for, and who it's not for. We're trying to attract only the most qualified responses we can get.

A Lesson On Fixed-Cost Media

Let's say you decide to buy some banner ad space. You're an affiliate for MOBE, so you use one of the banner ads we've already prepared for you. (Have I mentioned that we do almost everything for you?) Now, think of that same luxury shoe store from the previous section. Pretend you had $5,000 to spend on a billboard. You've got two options available in the same area, but one gets twice as many people walking past it every day than the other. You'd likely go for the one that got the most exposure, right?

Now, imagine you're writing the copy for the banner ad, trying to compel people to take action and come into your store (or for the online version, to click on your link). If you're paying a fixed cost to have the banner ad displayed, your goal here is to get as many actions as you possibly can. You don't care if some of the people responding to the ad and coming into your store aren't targeted leads. What difference does it make? You already paid the fixed price for banner ad space at the start of the month, so now you just want the maximum response you can get. You'd be willing to take those less targeted clicks, because who knows; you may be able to convert them later on. Your ad might look more like this:

> ## REVEALED: HOW TO HIRE TALENTED PEOPLE FAST, WITHOUT OVERPAYING!
> Free online videos reveal the secrets to posting
> ads, interviewing, and motivating a team ...
> **Click here** for our **free** video series.

Notice that the word "free" is used a lot more. There really is a free video training series after the lead opts in for the page we're promoting, so it's not a lie. The liberal use of the word "free" will attract people with no intention of paying for training later; but that's okay, because it will also attract some who can be persuaded to buy eventually, if we offer enough value and do enough follow up. So the next time you place an ad to generate traffic, ask yourself:

"Is my goal to attract only the most targeted leads possible, and actively screen out all the less targeted ones?"

Or...

"Is my goal to attract the maximum response possible, including targeted and untargeted leads, so I can follow up later and make sales?"

Offline Traffic Methods That Still Get Results

You probably know me best as an online marketer. But the truth is, I've invested *many* hundreds of thousands of dollars in radio ads and direct mail, and made millions of dollars in revenue as a result. I don't classify myself as an "online marketer," and neither should you. A better title is "direct response marketer." Why limit yourself to just the Internet, when there's so much money to be made offline too?

One of the earliest traffic methods I used when starting out was placing paper flyers on windshields of cars. It actually worked, and I got a $50 sale. About month later, that same customer bought a $1,700 program I was promoting, and I made a $1,000 commission on it. Now, I wouldn't recommend this strategy; it's very untargeted, and not very scalable. I'm sure you don't want to be the person posting flyers on people's windshields. But just to be clear: traffic can come from many different places; not just online. When people ask why I do offline marketing too, I tell them that people who don't go online much still like to buy things.

In fact, take a look at one of our direct mail ads I've invested hundreds of thousands of dollars on. You will see a copy on the next page.

I've sent these out all over America, and made millions of dollars in revenue from the leads they got us. Here's how it works: I get the postcards printed, usually 10,000+ at a time. We mail them out to people who live in the area surrounding the location of the live event, usually about 10 days before the event is scheduled to start. But we don't mail them to just anyone; this

Direct Mail ad we have used for one of our live events, the IM Freedom Workshop is performance-based media. We're interested in only spending money marketing to the most targeted leads we can get. I don't want to spend $0.90 sending a postcard to someone who never goes to seminars and has never spent money on one. So we rent a very targeted list of previous buyers of seminars like the one we're promoting. If they spent money on a course showing how to make money in real estate, there's a good possibility they're interested in making money through other vehicles, like online marketing.

We also target based on geography. When I first started promoting local seminars, I'd do stupid things like emailing several hundred thousand of my subscribers around the world about it. Do you really think someone from the UK is going to fly to California to come hear me speak for two hours? Of course not! I'm good, but I'm not that good. So now we're careful about targeting the right people geographically, and that's done by postal code. We only mail to people who live within a certain radius of the hotel where we're doing the seminar (such as four miles).

I might invest $15,000 to send these invitations out each time. Over time, I've scaled my advertising spending upward along with the increased revenue numbers—and you can do the same.

How To Avoid Getting Ripped Off When Buying Traffic

There are good traffic sources out there. But there are a lot more bad ones… and no shortage of people who will sell garbage traffic to newer affiliate marketers. And guess what? Even if I tell you about them, some of you will still get ripped off! With that said, I still occasionally buy ads from traffic vendors. Just let me give you some pointers so you can minimize the chances of this happening to you…

First of all—and I hate to use this line, because it's such a cliché—but if you're buying clicks, and the deal sounds too good to be true, then it probably is. If someone is trying to sell you 10,000 clicks for $5, then it's clearly a scam. There's no doubt about it. The clicks they're selling you are worthless, or they'd be charging you more for them. The clicks are likely generated by 'bots' (automated programs that click links just to rack up fake clicks). You'd think most people wouldn't be dumb enough to fall for these kind of deals; but you'd be surprised.

No one is going to sell you good traffic for such ridiculously low prices. Why would they? It makes no sense to sell a click for $0.05 if you can send it to another person's offer as an affiliate and make on average of $1.00 in revenue for yourself. So if the prices seem way too cheap, be exceedingly cautious. Typically, for genuine clicks you're going to pay from $0.55 / click and upwards. In some cases, you're better off buying clicks from someone who sells them for $2 per click over someone who sells them for $0.60 per click. The $2 clicks could be from people who are interested in your type of offer and right at the end of the buying process... basically with their 'credit card in hand.'

Also...be wary of buying traffic from other affiliate marketers promoting the same offers as you. Here's why: if they're in the business of sending clicks to earn commissions, then why would they sell you those clicks when they could keep them and earn the commissions themselves? Answer: they wouldn't. If they're selling you clicks, it's because they can make more money from *you.*

It will be tempting to buy some of this traffic, especially if the seller has made a lot of money promoting the same offers as you, and can show you big checks and screenshots of commissions they've supposedly got from this traffic. They may even give these traffic sources fancy names like 'Top Tier Premium Buyer Traffic.' It doesn't matter what they call it; most of the time, it's all the same traffic sources, which they paid pennies on the dollar for.

Now, for some of you reading this, it may sound hypocritical of me to be chastising affiliates for selling traffic, since I'm also in the traffic-selling business. I own several traffic agencies that sell clicks, including WeSellClicks.com. This is a completely separate company from MOBE, but a lot of MOBE affiliates get their traffic from there.

Why would I sell quality traffic to my own affiliates, when I could just send it to all to my own affiliate links and keep all the commissions myself?

Because I get something special in exchange for that traffic besides money: testimonials for our affiliate program. Those testimonials are like gold to me. I want more affiliates, so MOBE can grow to even higher heights. If I can help my new affiliates generate their first commissions by offering them a reliable traffic source, and then use their results in my marketing, that helps grow my company.

The Power of Tunnel Vision Focus

I want to end this chapter with a lesson about focus from Warren Buffett that will help you as an affiliate marketer.

My greatest idol when it comes to investing and making money is Warren Buffet. Ever since my mother bought me a book on him for Christmas and I read about this seemingly regular guy from Omaha, Nebraska who has accumulated billions of dollars over his lifetime, through the medium of investing, I've been fascinated with him. I've read dozens of books about him, spent many hours watching his videos on YouTube, and my thought process when it comes to multiplying money is based largely on his.

One of my favorite stories about Buffet was the time he met one of his fellow billionaires, Bill Gates, at a dinner. Gate's mother wanted the two to meet, though neither were particularly keen on the idea. Not because they didn't like each other, but because they didn't feel they'd have anything in common. Gates was the CEO of a fast-growing tech company. Buffet stayed well away from investing in tech companies, preferring to invest in businesses he felt he could understand. But upon meeting, the two hit it off, and the more they spoke the more fascinated they became with one another. They got on so well they virtually ignored all the other guests at the gathering! At dinner that night, Gate's mother asked the table to share what they thought the single greatest contributor to their success had been. Without missing a beat, both Gates and

Buffet (*by far the two most successful businessmen in the room*) replied at the same time, "Focus."

Making money online with affiliate marketing is really, really simple. So why do so few people do it? It's because the majority of those who try can't focus on one thing for long enough to see it work before they've moved on to the next.

This might sound like a contradiction, but one of the worst places to get high-leverage work done is in front of your computer. When you're online placing ads, you're also a prospect for thousands of other online businesses. They're competing for your attention with their ads, yelling, *"Hey, click here!"* Meanwhile, someone else is yelling, *"No, click here."* Another, *"Now click over here."* It's like being in a large crowd where everyone is calling your name. How can you possibly focus in that environment?

I'm not suggesting you should try to make money with affiliate marketing without going online. That'd be silly. I'm just saying that when you do sit down in front of your computer to build your business, you should have a very clear and definitive purpose in mind. Your thought process should be along the lines of, *"I'm going to place five new ads using this one traffic method in the next 60 minutes. I'm not going to check my email, Facebook, or go on Skype. I'm going to have tunnel vision, only for the task at hand: placing ads, and driving traffic to the offer I'm promoting."*

You must learn to focus on the task at hand, and do one important thing at a time. When I'm trying to really focus (like I am right now, writing this book), I work in concentrated blocks of time. If I can do my work without needing to be online, I'll also turn off my Wi-Fi so I can't even be tempted. I'll turn on a one-hour countdown timer on my iPhone (which is also put in Airplane Mode), and then just focus on the task at hand. That's how I'm able to get the important things done in my business.

Most new affiliate marketers don't operate that way. Instead, they sit down at their computer with no clarity in mind about what task they want to accomplish, with no clear amount of time allocated to the task—and with no real purpose. Before they have to think too hard, they go check their email. And so it begins. Three hours later, after watching endless marketing videos from the 20 different marketing gurus, checking photos of their friends and their friend's pets on Facebook, and wasting time on to YouTube, they look at their watch and think, *"Wow, where did the time go?"*

They've been very busy for those three hours, but haven't been even slightly productive.

You need to constantly ask yourself, "Is what I'm doing right now moving my business forward? Is what I'm doing right now going to lead to more customers, or increase the value of the customers I already have?" If you can't answer those questions with a resounding "Yes!" then you probably shouldn't be doing that task.

Here's the difficult part about this for new affiliate marketers: you don't always know which tasks actually bring in the money. After all, you've never made money online before, so you don't have the actual cause-and-effect experience. Let me make it simple for you: ***You drive targeted traffic (clicks) to your affiliate link in significant quantities.*** That's it. You do this by placing ads in front of the right people, and enticing them to click the ad through your ad copy.

For example, let's say you have a really bad toothache. You're in agony—you can't think about anything else except the pain. So you go online and search for a solution, and two ads from two different local dentists (each equally capable of treating you) come up:

WIDE RANGE OF DENTIST SERVICES AVAILABLE
All dentist services offered, including cosmetic and corrective dentistry.

and

GOT AN AGONIZING TOOTHACHE RIGHT NOW?

Get instant relief! Visit us today, right now, and we'll take the pain away. **Click here** to book your appointment…

Which of these two ads are you most likely to click on?

Take note, because this is important: When you're placing ads, your goal is NOT to get a sale. Your main goal is to get the click, so don't start talking about the product or service in the ad—that can come later. There are exceptions to this rule, but that's a more advanced strategy for when you have more experience. For now, your ads should be written with the express purpose of getting a click, period. The two best ways to get a click are (1) to offer a big, outrageous benefit, or (2) create curiosity that can only be resolved through clicking the ad and seeing what it's about.

Here's an example of using curiosity in an ad, for a product about saving money:

A TWO-STEP TECHNIQUE TO SAVE MONEY

This simple mistake is costing you a minimum of $50 a day. **Click here** to avoid it…

What's the first thought that goes through your mind when reading that ad? I'll bet it's, "What's the two-step technique? What simple mistake could I be making that's costing me $50 a day?" Well, how do you find out?

You have to click.

CHAPTER FIVE

The Origins of the MOBE High Ticket Affiliate Program

S o far, we've covered a lot of ground in this book. I've talked about what makes a good business model, why affiliate marketing is the best business model, how to get started as an affiliate marketer, and how to send cold traffic.

I've also mentioned my very successful MOBE high ticket affiliate program several times, including a few of our many success stories. Now, I want to dedicate a full chaptnicer to MOBE and the MOBE high ticket affiliate program, including the origins of the company and how I went from humble beginnings on a farm in Australia to the helm of a $100 million business that's poised to spring toward the billion dollar mark

In this chapter, you'll learn:

- **Where MOBE Is Today:** One of the best affiliate programs on the planet.

- **My Humble Beginnings:** How I went from mowing lawns to creating my own affiliate program.

- **The Turning Point:** The decision to create a program that gives the average affiliate (*even ones with very little experience*) everything they need to get commissions of up to $1,000 (or more) per sale.

- **Why MOBE Pays Such Generous Commissions To Its Affiliates**

Let's get started...

MOBE Today - One Of The Best Affiliate Programs On The Planet

Today, MOBE is a very successful affiliate program. Even my competitors would admit it's one of the best in the world. But that's not enough for me. I want MOBE to be the best affiliate program in the world by a large margin, and I won't stop until I've achieved that. With that said, I'm VERY proud of what MOBE has accomplished so far and where we are today.

Currently, MOBE offers lots of different products, services, and live events (including the Titanium, Platinum, and Diamond Masterminds). Every month, we generate a lot of traffic to our websites - *millions* of clicks. Lots

HTAM CASE STUDY

Lack of Computer Skills Not An Issue for Older Canadian Man Who Earns $10,094 with the MOBE high ticket affiliate program

My name is Guy Tomlinson. I live in Calgary, Alberta, Canada and started with MOBE to finance my retirement. To date, I've made $10,094 in commissions through the MOBE high ticket affiliate program even though I had zero computer skills when I started.

Before MOBE, I had 40+ years in sales, but on a person-to-person basis. I had never used the computer much. After joining MOBE, the training and coach helped me through the learning curve. To date, I've made $10,094 and continue to buy traffic and follow up with those leads. This is just the start of my journey to be able to provide for my retirement.

Guy Tomlinson (Platinum Member)

of microsecond actions of index fingers on mouses, connected to millions of potential buyers. Lots of people looking at their computer screens, clicking ads that connect to our websites, where we can sell them valuable training products and make good money. This is what enables us to pay out *millions* of dollars every month to the affiliates who place the ads.

Despite the huge sums of money we pay out to our thousands of affiliates, my goal is to one day have millions of them; there's easily enough of you out there. These people promote our various websites. Some of them come to us and know what they're doing; they have a lot of experience with generating traffic, and within just a few years of promoting MOBE have generated millions of dollars. Our Number One affiliate is actually a team of four guys who, in the last two and a half years, have generated over $8,000,000 in revenue. But many of our affiliates are brand-new, so we train them on how to go place ads and generate traffic, and do whatever we can to make their job easier. After all, we have a huge incentive; the more successful they are and the more money they make, the more money we'll make.

Every two weeks when I pay all of MOBE's affiliates, which usually amounts to over $500,000 leaving our bank accounts, I actually enjoy it. Really, I do. I like seeing that amount go higher and higher, because it means that MOBE is making more money—and it's still growing.

One of the things that's driven me from the very start was my desire to create an affiliate program in our niche that paid out more money than any other. I wanted my affiliates to be paid and treated so well that they wouldn't even think about promoting something else—although unlike other programs, I let them do that if they want. In fact, not only do my affiliates get paid generous commissions, I offer them other perks too, just to keep them loyal—like covering the costs of their own luxury car. Over the years, dozens of MOBE affiliates have been able to drive Ferraris, BMWs, Jeeps, Mercedes, Jaguars... and we even recently had a guy pick up a brand-new Tesla. This is part of the MOBE Motors program, which you can see at **www.mobemotors.com**. Go check out the website, and you'll see videos of every one of these people and the cars they've been able to get through placing ads for MOBE.

I also pay out over $100,000 every month in a High Performers Cash Bonus program to my very top affiliates, just as a "thank you" for their continued support. And as I write these words, I'm four days away from getting on a plane and flying to Florida, to get on a four-night cruise down to Mexico and back with my top MOBE affiliates. MOBE will be paying for it all, as a thank you to our affiliates who've generated over $100,000 with our program—and there's a whole bunch of them!

Anyone who's made over $1 million with the MOBE high ticket affiliate program (currently there are five of them) also gets to come to our international training events held at five-star resorts all around the world, in places like Fiji, the Bahamas, Costa Rica, Thailand, etc..... and MOBE pays for it all.

MOBE has some of the best affiliates in the world, but it hasn't been easy to reach this level. It all started when I decided to go from being an affiliate marketer to being a company owner with a great affiliate program. As much as I loved affiliate marketing, I always liked the idea of working with hundreds or even thousands of affiliates, and leveraging their efforts (in exchange for commissions) to amplify my own. I knew that with the help of affiliates, together we'd be able to reach the masses. Little did I know it was the hardest thing I'd ever do, in a life full of hard work. I'm a hard worker, but I'll be straight with you: if I had known just how hard creating my own company would be, I probably wouldn't have done it.

But I'm glad I did.

My Humble Beginnings: From Mowing Lawns to Living Large

Back in mid-2008, I was living in Dalkeith, one of the wealthiest suburbs in Perth—though I certainly wasn't rich back then. Most of the homes on the street I lived on were worth $2 million and upwards. Meanwhile, I was living out the back of one of them, in what we call in Australia a "granny flat" belonging to the owner of the house, Les. Les was a retired mining engineer who'd occasionally do consulting and get paid $2,000 a day. It's funny now, but

I used to be so incredibly impressed with that amount of money! He was also a heavy chain-smoker and alcoholic, and he passed away a few months after I moved out. I remember he could tell how hungry I was, and always used to always tell me, *"Matthew, your last shirt has no pockets."* In other words, *"You can't take the money with you."* They're wise words I try not to forget.

Each day I'd go to university and take my classes. By then, I'd changed my degree about three times. Starting with a double degree in psychology and philosophy, I'd ended up studying finance and accounting... and although I got half-decent grades, I was a lousy student. I was too impatient to study; I wanted to get out there and start earning!

My favorite movie back then (and still to this day) was Oliver Stone's *Wall Street.* I was actually watching it again last night, as I write this. All young guys who want to go into finance usually want to be like Gordon Gekko, the corporate raider and multimillionaire slick businessman. Even though he's the bad guy in the movie, there's a certain irresistible temptation to his character. The suits, the cigars, the limousines, the women... I can almost quote that entire movie line for line, I've seen it so many times.

Even back then, I wanted to be rich.

Growing up on a farm and seeing my parents struggle financially had taught me one thing: I did not want to have to struggle myself. So at the age of 21, I decided I wanted to become a billionaire someday. That seemed about the furthest thing from struggling I could think of. I figured that before I set my aim on making that first billion, though, I should focus on making $100,000 before the end of the year. That way, I'd have some money to invest, and with the amount of time I had left to live—based on the average life expectancy of men being about 84, and the inevitable medical advances over the next 60 years—I figured I could live to at least 100.

"That means I've got about 80 years of capital growth," I figured. If I could invest that $100k to give me a 20% return every year (which I based on what Warren Buffet had been able to do), not touch the principal, and reinvest the interest, then that would make me about $216 billion by the time I hit the century

mark. Of course, I would need to take into account inflation and maybe a few bad years, but with those numbers, I was sure I'd hit the big billion at least.

The naivety of me thinking I could match the investing returns of the world's greatest investor is laughable in hindsight. But that's one of the advantages of being young when you start a business; you have this foolish and optimistic confidence about what you can accomplish, and are not overrun by the fear of what might go wrong (which often comes with age). So I set my sights on making that first $100k—and it became an obsession for me. On a piece of paper, I typed:

> *"I will have a net worth of $100,000 by December 31st, 2008."*
> *"I will have a net worth of $100,000 by December 31st, 2008."*
> *"I will have a net worth of $100,000 by December 31st, 2008."*
> *"I will have a net worth of $100,000 by December 31st, 2008."*
> *"I will have a net worth of $100,000 by December 31st, 2008"*
> *"I will have a net worth of $100,000 by December 31st, 2008."*
> *"I will have a net worth of $100,000 by December 31st, 2008."*
> *"I will have a net worth of $100,000 by December 31st, 2008."*
> *"I will have a net worth of $100,000 by December 31st, 2008."*
> *"I will have a net worth of $100,000 by December 31st, 2008."*

I printed off a few copies and put it on my bathroom mirror and on the wall next to my desk. I even stuck it on the ceiling above my bed so I'd see it every morning when I woke up. I thought about it all the time.

Now, at the time I was making about $15 an hour. About a year prior, I'd started a little part-time gardening/house cleaning business called 'Home Helpers.' I had one employee (me), and my head office was my bedroom. I got my first client by printing off a few hundred flyers and sticking them in people's mailboxes. I got ONE response. One. But I did a great job weeding this man's garden, and from there, I started asking for referrals for his neighbors. Soon, I had more clients than I could handle.

It wasn't terrible work, though it wasn't pleasant either. Some days I'd be mowing lawns. Other days, digging a big tree stump out of the ground. Next, cleaning swimming pools. If the homeowner wanted me to pick up their dog's 'business' off their lawn, I'd do it. I was paid cash, and every single day I did a job I'd walk into the bank branch on campus and deposit whatever I'd made. The type of bank account I was using was one of those high-interest ones where you get penalized every time you make a withdrawal. So for several years, money only ever went *into* that account. It never came out.

The work was steady—the homeowners saw how hard I worked, and I made sure they always got really good value for their money. Between my studies, I was working just about full time making all the cash I possibly could. I didn't know it at the time, but my financial thermostat was set so low that I was being grossly underpaid. For some of the more manual work, I could have been getting three times that, especially in that suburb. But I enjoyed being my own boss, at least.

The main problem was the $15 an hour part. I calculated how long it was going to take to save up $100,000 in cash, and it was literally years. I didn't have the patience for that, and it was seriously going to mess up my plans to make that first billion. The breaking point happened one day when I went into someone's home to clean their bathroom, and they'd left an enormous surprise for me right in their toilet bowl. Probably not intentionally (at least I hope not). But whoever that was, if you're reading this, *thank you*. You were the inspiration for me making the decision to quit cleaning houses and doing other people's gardening.

I had to come up with some other way to make money, and fast. The year was rapidly coming to an end, and I needed to reach that first $100,000. So I sat down at my computer, went to Google, and typed in "how to make money online." Little did I know that that innocent search would completely change my life. If not for those five words, who knows how my life would have turned out?

To make a long story short, I ended up clicking someone's ad, becoming a lead for them, and buying a $2,000 moneymaking program. I had no clue what I was doing in the beginning, but I was resourceful, and I was motivated. If I didn't know how to do something, I went and found the answers. For those first few months I treated my business like a hobby. It was a hobby I took seriously, but it was still just a hobby. A few months later, I invested the rest of my life savings, along with what I could borrow (a total of $38,000), and that was when I got real serious.

I was going to need to learn how to place ads on the Internet to get people to my website. So I caught the bus into the city, went to a bookstore, and charged almost $500 worth of books to my Visa credit card. I ended up reading just one of them, and not even finishing it. It was called *Google AdWords for Dummies*, by Howie Jacobson. Flicking through the pages on the bus ride home, I immediately felt discouraged, thinking, *"This looks waaay too technical for me. I don't think I'll be able to do this."* But I decided to just start at Chapter One, and work my way through it page by page.

Then, at the end of each chapter, I'd actually go do whatever was being taught. And that's the first big lesson I'm going to give you: if you want to actually make money after finishing this book, start taking action now. Not when you get to the end, but right now. Go join a great affiliate program like what MOBE offers at least. Be one of the few people who actually implement. For every hour you spend reading, spend 5 applying.

Back to the story. Soon, I was driving steady traffic to my website each day. At least 20 people were clicking my ads daily. A small percentage were actually filling out the form on my capture page (which I'd paid a website company $400 to build because I didn't know how). I'd then call them, with the sales script the company provided next to my computer, and try to fumble my way through it before I was cut off or hung up on. I think the longest conversation I had in that first month may have clocked in at 30 seconds. But the more I failed, the more determined I became. As an entrepreneur, being stubborn can be a good thing.

The company I was with didn't provide any real training to its affiliates, and since I was so new to technical things, I decided to get help. I went down to my local university, and posted a few flyers on billboards that said I was looking for a computer science student who could build more website pages for me, and just show me how to do basic things. I ended up getting an Iranian guy called Kia (we're still friends to this day) to come work for me for 2-3 hours a week, and I'd pay him about $15 / hour. I'd sit next to him in front of my computer, and tell him how I wanted my website pages to look. And then he'd build them.

Here's a picture of me in my "office" back then, which he took:

On the next page is my first real 'ad' I ever wrote, which because I didn't know how to advertise online, I put up at the local super market on a billboard.

I'd go check the flyer each day and see if anyone had torn off any of the phone numbers. When I saw one or two missing, I'd get excited and think someone was going to call me and I'd be able to make a sale... but no one ever did.

After 9 months in, I still hadn't made a dime. Literally, not a single dollar. I didn't get too upset at the company, as I knew it was my own fault. I just needed to develop the necessary skills—like lead generation, honing my sales

chops, and focusing on important revenue-generating tasks during my work hours—and then I'd be able to get results.

But it became increasingly frustrating—and my own self-image (as an entrepreneur) was becoming very fragile. Finally, I got my first sale, and it felt GOOD. I made a $1,000 commission. For the next two years, I had a few more good days, like the one in late Feb 2010, when I had a customer go "all in" with that company's products, and get the two back-end programs I was promoting—which netted me $15,200. But those days were extremely rare; I could count them on one hand. The majority were quiet "earn-nothing" days. Most months, I was lucky to clear a few thousand dollars.

This was my full-time income source, so the money didn't go very far. For the amount of time and effort I was putting in, I couldn't help but ask, is all this really worth it? Should I just quit, go back to university, finish my degree, and get a job? That's what everyone around me was telling me to do.

Long after the evidence of my results suggested I wasn't cut out for this business, I was still persistent. What kept me going was the stories. The stories of everyday people who were making fortunes in Internet marketing. I'd hear about them, and it gave me hope. Hope that even after two years of inconsistent and mediocre results, that one day, things would be different. I drew inspiration from those stories. They fueled my fire, and I decided to persist. That's one reason I include so many success stories in this book and on our MOBE affiliate websites; every time my affiliates think about giving up, I want them to see what they are potentially throwing away. In fact, there's a whole Appendix full of success stories in the back of this book.

The Turning Point: A Program That Finally Gives Average Affiliates Everything They Need

The MOBE revolution began when I quit the company I'd started with. *"Someone who's new to this business shouldn't have to go through all I went through,"* I told myself. I wanted to create an affiliate program that anyone could join, and by following the step-by-step training, could have a real chance of success with. And I wanted to sell only training programs that were truly valuable, and showed people exactly what they needed to do.

A huge motivation was all the flaws of the first affiliate program I had joined. And there were a lot of them. First off, the leadership didn't do enough to help the affiliates make money promoting their products. As I've already mentioned, the affiliate had to do everything: create their own websites, call their leads and do the sales, write email follow-up campaigns, provide all the support to their new customers—everything. And honestly, the products themselves were lousy. I could see that right away when the first one I bought from them arrived at my doorstop, and I discovered a few CDs and one DVD in an oversized box. It looked like they had spent more time making the box look nice, than the actual product. For new affiliate marketers like me, who had never done any of this before, success was extremely hard, and the failure rate was incredibly high. I remember going to one of the first live events for that company back in Sydney in early 2009; there must have been 200 people in that room, minimum. I'd be surprised if today, just 10 of the original people in that room are still involved in the business. Heck, I might be the ONLY one.

But all that pain and effort was worth it in the end. I didn't know it then, but being an affiliate for that company was the ultimate training ground for me to create my own affiliate program. I got to see firsthand what affiliates needed to do well, and also what mistakes to avoid.

Not surprisingly, the company I started with eventually went out of business. The co-founders had disagreements, and one was forced out (which is one of the reasons I refuse to have equity-level business partners; rarely do they work out in the long term). So in 2011, after that company was finished, I had a thought... "What if someone actually did this *right?*" With the blind confidence of a 23-year-old kid who'd never ran a big company before, I decided that someone was going to be me!

That's when I decided to start MOBE, which stands for My Online Business Education. The company is meant to be just that: a business owner's online business education training—meaning they can access our training from anywhere in the world, and get training in any area of their business they need. Whether they need help with increasing sales, hiring, scaling, launching marketing campaigns, honing their sales presentation skills, or whatever area of business you can think of, we've got them covered.

I also decided to create an amazing affiliate program, so regular people could earn commissions promoting our programs from home. My big advantage was I had spent the last three years learning just about every challenge affiliates could have, as well as what actually worked. I found myself constantly asking, "What if someone who had been an affiliate marketer themselves and actually knew what it was like, was to create a program that gave the average affiliate (even the ones with very little experience) everything they needed to get commissions of up to (and over) $1,000 per sale?"

I implemented that idea with a single-minded focus… and all false modesty aside, that's part of the reason why MOBE affiliates have earned over $51 million in total commissions to date, with many of them transforming their lives. With the way MOBE is set up, affiliates can get paid *more* money for promoting us than just about any other company out there.

Why Does MOBE Pay Such Generous Commissions to Its Affiliates?

What makes the MOBE high ticket affiliate program truly unique is the back end, and the fact that buyers are locked to you for life. Most affiliate programs don't pay you on the back end. And with the very few that do, buyers are not locked to you. That means you could generate a $100 buyer for a company, and earn somewhere around a $50 commission. And then, six months later, suppose that $100 customer decides to buy a $2,000 program from that same company. If another affiliate promoted that $2,000 program to your buyer, and they got the last click, they would get the $1,000 commission.

I've always had a problem with that model. So when I created the MOBE high ticket affiliate program, I created the rule that once you refer a paying customer to us, that customer is locked to you *for life*. And here's the best part: our follow-up isn't just for 30 days, or 90 days, or even a year. It's forever. Ten years from now, MOBE will still be finding additional ways to help our existing clients build better and more successful businesses. And every time we do, some affiliate will still be getting paid a commission on *every single one* of their purchases.

The best commissions to make are the big ones you don't see coming. I don't know about you, but if I'm an affiliate marketer, that's an amazing proposition.

Now, you may be wondering why other affiliate programs don't operate on the same principles. It's simple: backwards thinking and greed. Other program owners think that if they cut the affiliate in on the back-end sales, there won't be enough money left for them. But don't go thinking I'm some kind of altruistic saint just yet; there's greed on my part too.

I know that if I pay my affiliates really well for their traffic and also pay them on all back-end sales, then they'll send a lot more traffic to MOBE instead of the competition. So long as MOBE pays them the most money for their traffic, they'll usually send it our way. And even though paying out enormous commissions results in smaller margins for us, we make up for it in volume.

Affiliates receiving their checks on stage at the Super Charge Summit in London

MOBE Has One of the Most Generous Compensation Plans in the Industry

Diamond member Darren Salkeld with Matt Lloyd at the Super Charge Summit Las Vegas

Diamond member Shaqir Hussyin with Matt Lloyd at the Super Charge Summit Sydney

The MOBE High Ticket Affiliate Marketing Program has paid out over $51 million to regular people (like you) in 37 countries around the world and we're just getting started. Join us at **www.fivefigureaffiliatemarketing.com**

Diamond member Adeline Sugianto with Matt Lloyd at the Super Charge Summit Sydney

Diamond member Ernest Lim with Matt Lloyd at the Super Charge Summit Sydney

Diamond member Georg Kerschhackl with Matt Lloyd at the Super Charge Summit London

Diamond member Deborah Robertson with Matt Lloyd at the Super Charge Summit Las Vegas

The MOBE High Ticket Affiliate Marketing Program has paid out over $51 million to regular people (like you) in 37 countries around the world and we're just getting started. Join us at **www.fivefigureaffiliatemarketing.com**

MOBE Affiliates Are Also Rewarded With Many Additional Cash and Prizes Including a Vehicle of Their Choice Through the MOBE Motors Program.

Diamond member John Chow with his family and second MOBE Motors, a Jaguar F Type v8 S

Diamond member Nick Pratt with his BMW Z4 MOBE Motors

Visit www.mobemotors.com for more success stories and videos and learn how you too can get the vehicle of your dreams paid for by MOBE.

Diamond members Bill and Michelle Pescosolido with their MOBE Motors

Diamond member Ryan Jaten chose a boat for his MOBE Motors Vehicle

The MOBE High Ticket Affiliate Marketing Program has paid out over $51 million to regular people (like you) in 37 countries around the world and we're just getting started. Join us at www.fivefigureaffiliatemarketing.com

Diamond members John Chow, Brian Price, Shaqir Hussyin, Carolina Millan, Bill & Michelle Pescosolido, Terry Lamb, Zach Crawford and Darren Salkeld receiving their 6 and 7 figure ring awards from Matt Lloyd at the Titanium Mastermind Bahamas.

Some of our Platinum and Diamond members enjoying the MOBE Leader's Cruise 2015 including: Georg Kerschhackl, Franka Peels, Carolina Millan, Paul O'Mahony, Susan Geer Zanghi, Chris Rowell, MeiDee Lim, Ryan Jaten, Terry Lamb and some of their guests.

Diamond and Platinum members John Chow, Michael Morin, Terry Lamb and Matt Dreier receiving cash prizes at the Titanium Mastermind in Cabo San Lucas. Other members collecting prizes on behalf of Sue Smart and Zach Crawford. Total cash prizes awarded: $50,000!

Platinum member Nancy Showalter receiving her Award of Excellence at the Titanium Mastermind Thailand.

The MOBE High Ticket Affiliate Marketing Program has paid out over $51 million to regular people (like you) in 37 countries around the world and we're just getting started. Join us at www.fivefigureaffiliatemarketing.com

MOBE Affiliate Partners Have Fun and Enjoy a Great Support System with Coaching, Sales Support, Customer Support and a Thriving Community of Likeminded Entrepreneurs.

Titanium Mastermind Phuket, Thailand

Visit www.mobe.com/mastermindschedule to view dates and locations
for upcoming masterminds.

Diamond Mastermind Bali

Platinum Mastermind Curaçao

The MOBE High Ticket Affiliate Marketing Program has paid out over $51 million to
regular people (like you) in 37 countries around the world and we're just getting started.
Join us at **www.fivefigureaffiliatemarketing.com**

Dolphin Adventure at the Titanium Mastermind Puerto Vallarta, Mexico.

Diamond member Carolina Millan getting ready to drive around a race track, one of the many fun activities attendees enjoyed at the Diamond Mastermind Cancun, Mexico.

Diamond members Frank Torchia, Deborah Robertson, Becca Barry, Carolina Millan and Adam Holland enjoying some water sports at the Diamond Mastermind Cancun, Mexico.

Entertainment at the farewell dinner Titanium Mastermind Phuket, Thailand

Titanium Mastermind members enjoying an elephant ride in Phuket, Thailand

Diamond Mastermind members enjoying a boat cruise in Cancun, Mexico

CHAPTER SIX

How To Join The MOBE High Ticket Affiliate Program And Your 90-Day Action Plan

I f you're still reading, congratulations! You made it past the half-way mark. You're one of the very few (maybe less than 5% of people) who got this book and actually read it this far.

You're also in that category of people who achieve the majority of the results (and get to make the most money). It's ironic to me that most people give up before they have started, because they think it will be too hard. They say it's lonely at the top, and they're right, because there are so few people up here. Most give up long before they get here, and it's a shame, because it's honestly not as hard as they think.

So where to go from here?

You're going to continue the momentum you've gained so far and finish reading this book, and then go on to transform your life just like hundreds of my top MOBE affiliates have.

But FIRST... before you read another word of this book, I want you to join the MOBE high ticket affiliate program.

After you join the MOBE high ticket affiliate program, continue reading this book while implementing the 90 Day Action Plan in this chapter. Once you

---

Get access to the ultimate HTAM (High Ticket Affiliate Marketing) system, which pays you up to $13,500 per sale at **www.fivefigureaffiliatemarketing.com**. You will also be assigned a personal HTAM coach, who will walk you through a simple, 21 step training program that shows you how to get started.

HTAM CASE STUDY

MOBE Coach Helps Ernest Lim From Singapore Support Family With Income From the MOBE high ticket affiliate program

My name is Ernest Lim. I grew up in Singapore, but now live in Sydney, Australia with my wife and our three children. I've been in the MOBE high ticket affiliate program for 2 years and have earned over $106,087 to date! I'm able to support my family with this income and pay the bills and mortgage without working for a company.

Looking back to when my second child was born, my wife had to leave her job to be a full-time mother. My job at the time – as a manufacturing engineer in a printing technology company – wasn't enough to pay the bills and mortgage. I considered going back to university, but that would have been costly and taken years and didn't guarantee a higher-paying job. So I started attending events to learn how to make money as an entrepreneur (even though I always had an employee mindset). I struggled for 2 years and was on the verge of giving up when I found MOBE. The business model reminded me of a well-engineered car with a powerful engine. All I had to do was put in the key and learn how to drive.

I picked up new advertising skills from MOBE's coaches and applied what I learned. 5 weeks later, I made my first commission of $8,088. I had never made so much money online in 1 day before! What made it real for me, though, was when Matt Lloyd called me to congratulate me personally. Now, after 2 years, I've made a total of $106,087 with the MOBE high ticket affiliate program. I've worked the system hard to get to this point, but it's been worth every minute.

Ernest Lim (Diamond Member)

implement the plan, I'd like to hear from you personally. **But only once you've made it through the 90 days.** My private email address is workwithmattlloyd@gmail.com. I may or may not respond to your email, but I assure you—it will be seen by me. But please: only contact me after you've done the 90 days. I like to work with those who can commit to their success and follow through. And the next time you attend a live MOBE training event like the Titanium Mastermind, make sure to introduce yourself.

Step 1: Join The MOBE High Ticket Affiliate Program

I've told you a lot about the MOBE high ticket affiliate program and how it has paid out a documented $51 million to people in 37 countries all over the world so far.

Now… $51 million is a LOT of money, but that's just the beginning. The business training niche is an *enormous* niche and this is just a drop in the ocean. You always hear people say, *"I wish I got in on that early"* when they talk about a stock, investment, or opportunity. Well, now is still early for MOBE.

When you join the MOBE high ticket affiliate program, you will get instant access to the same program that has paid out $51 million to affiliates.

You will also get a 21-step training program that will walk you through some of the things we've talked about in this book (but in even greater detail). You'll learn how to apply the HTAM Method and get commissions of up to $13,500 deposited into your bank account just for sending cold traffic (as a level 1 affiliate).

You will also get your own personal coach.

When you join the MOBE high ticket affiliate program, you'll get access to a real person, an online marketing expert, that will answer your questions. Your personal coach will help you through the 21 steps, and hold you accountable and motivate you when needed.

Why?

Because like I've said many times, I've been where you are. The first affiliate program I joined didn't provide any training or coaching to its affiliates. The MOBE high ticket affiliate program is different. It's designed to give you every-thing you need to generate high-ticket sales and get big commissions… which benefits me in the long run too.

So, join the MOBE high ticket affiliate program right now. Go to:

www.fivefigureaffiliatemarketing.com

Step 2: Implement Your 90-Day Action Plan

Day 1: On Day 1 (today), join the MOBE high ticket affiliate program at www.fivefigureaffiliatemarketing.com (You should have just done this)

Days 1-7: Over the next week, continue reading this book while going through the 21-step training and working with your coach. The second half of this book is more advanced, but it will give you valuable insight into how to be a successful affiliate marketer, and is worth finishing now.

Days 2-21: For the next 21 days, minimum, one of my coaches will be working with you. You'll need to invest at least 40 minutes of your time each day (which anyone who is even half-serious about building a real business should be willing to do). Ideally, you should dedicate more time (on top of this 40 minutes per day) to self-education. Find time to read this book, learn more about MOBE and our products, read inspirational stories, and do more research on affiliate marketing in general. Even if you are already knowl-edgeable about affiliate marketing, consider broadening and deepening your education, or even tweaking and tightening your niche.

Day 22-35: Start placing your first ads and selling through your affiliate links, but only AFTER clearly identifying your target market and niche. If you're not ready by this point, then you haven't been working hard enough, and you haven't been taking this opportunity seriously enough.

Day 36-49: Invest your profits in more ads and clicks using the strategies taught in Chapter 4. Carefully track where each sale comes from (it's easy to add tracking to your ads)... and remember this crucial point: *Focus on only one advertising method, or you'll dilute your effectiveness.*

Day 50-63: Continue to measure your results. One simple way to measure them is through dollars; track how much each advertisement or offer earns you. Feed the stallions and starve the ponies.

Stop using the ads that fail to bring in a profit, and double down (or more) on those that do. Invest the profits, buying more traffic with the additional income.

Day 64-90: Experiment with new ad sources. Keep feeding the stallions and starving the ponies, especially as the value of your ads change. Remember, not all ads remain effective as time passes. However, treat your profitable ads like valuable assets, even if you're tired of them.

NOTE: Just because you're tired of seeing your ad, doesn't mean your prospects are. As long as it keeps bringing in money it's a good ad, and your prospects obviously aren't tired of it yet! Some ads will run profitably for years (even decades).

Day 91: Email me with the details of your story!

The MOBE High Ticket Affiliate Program is the world's best HTAM system that pays you up to $13,500 per sale!

Backend high-ticket sales are made FOR YOU: MOBE does the work and deposits commissions directly into your bank account twice a month!

PLUS ... you get a **personal coach** that will walk you through a simple 21-step training program on how to make your first BIG commission (even if you have zero computer skills!)

90% of the work required to run a business is Done For You:

- ✓ No products to create
- ✓ No fulfillment or customer service
- ✓ No payment processing
- ✓ No website design or hosting
- ✓ No sales presentations or funnels to create
- ✓ No selling in person or over the phone
- ... It's all Done For You!

Join today at: **www.fivefigureaffiliatemarketing.com**

CHAPTER SEVEN

How To Get To The Next Level With "Warm" Traffic

A fter generating cold traffic as a Level 1 Affiliate, the next level is sending warm traffic. This is where you build an email list of subscribers to follow up with. At this stage, you'll develop a relationship with your email list, making them more likely to trust you when you recommend a product. It's called "warm" traffic because they have a relationship with you (whereas with cold traffic, they don't know who you are). When you have your own responsive list like this, you have the power to send traffic to an offer in large quantities just by clicking the Send button on a broadcast email.

In time, your email list will become an asset, one that allows you to create Income-On-Demand with virtually no effort. For me, with the MOBE email list, whenever I push "send," it can generate thousands of dollars (even tens of thousands of dollars). It's kind of like being a famous songwriter that can write a hit song at will.

In fact, John Lennon used to joke with his friend and songwriter partner, Paul McCartney, *"Okay! Today let's write a swimming pool."* With his fan base and his remarkable ability to write popular songs, Lennon could produce all the money he needed ***on demand.***

Having a responsive email list is like having an ATM in your home that you can continually receive money from. It takes time to develop and manage, but when you master it, the potential for income is (virtually) limitless.

Monetize your email list by leveraging my proven Done-For-You sales process that sells your leads into high-ticket offers and pays you big commissions of up to $13,500 per sale! Get started now at **www.fivefigureaffiliatemarketing.com**.

In this chapter, you'll learn how to build, nurture, and monetize an email list, including:

* **The Power Is In Your Relationship With Your List:** The key is to provide value, recommend good offers, and be a trusted advisor.

* **How to Build a Strong Relationship With Your List and Make Maximum Profits**

* **What NOT To Do In Your Email Marketing:** These mistakes will burn your list and they'll never buy from you again.

* **Automated Email Follow Up Sequences:** This is one of the most powerful (and easiest) email marketing strategies, and it can increase sales by up to 30% or more.

* **How to Build Your Own 'Money Getting' List**

* **MOBE Case Study: The 'Masturbation Email'** (And How It Cost Me A Car)

* **How to Write Profit-Pulling Emails:** You don't need to be a great writer to write emails that sell (just follow these simple rules...)

* **How To Get An Instant Influx Of Cash With Broadcast Emails**

* **How To Double Sales With Segmentation [Advanced]**

* **Why Getting Good at Conversions Will "Extract" Money From Your List**

* **Even MORE Ways To Extract Money From Your List**

Let's get started...

The Power Is In Your *Relationship* With Your List

It's taken me years, but I've built a very strong relationship with my email list. If I were an affiliate for someone, for example, I could send 5,000 people to that person's website in a few hours very easily. If their website was selling something of value for my subscribers and I heavily endorsed it, I could make tens of thousands of dollars from that single email. But keep this in mind: I've built my email list over seven years, and I've invested a lot of time into establishing trust with my subscribers. I've also spent a lot of money on all the traffic I've bought. Don't expect to get to this stage any time soon; and don't try to rush it before you're ready. But do realize it is very possible to make 6 figures a year with an affiliate marketing business, even if you have a tiny list.

One of my affiliates, Andrea Goodsaid of Gainesville, Florida has a tiny list of less than a few thousand subscribers which she's built up over the years—and she's made over $184,000 in commissions in the last few years promoting MOBE, because she's created such strong relationships with her subscribers. Not only does she respond to them when they reach out to her, she brings them into her Facebook groups, answers their questions, shows them she genuinely cares, and even invites them to come meet her while attending live events. The important thing is that you build a relationship with that list, and position yourself as the expert and trusted advisor they listen to.

A solid recommendation from someone you trust (*and who has no reason to mislead you*) to go buy something is one of the most powerful forms of marketing in the world. Imagine a new restaurant has just opened in your area. You've seen their billboards all over town, heard their radio ads, and even gotten some of their flyers in the mail. They may have spent tens of thousands of dollars on all that marketing, and yet you still don't go there and buy a meal. It's not that you're not interested, it's just that in the sea of marketing you swim through on a daily basis, there's not a big enough reason for you to eat there anytime soon.

But then one day, your neighbor (who also happens to be a friend) starts chatting with you. After a few minutes of small talk, they tell you about the amazing experience they had last night at this restaurant. They tell you about how good the food was, how nice the atmosphere is, and how it's going to be their new spot for social get-togethers. A few nights later, when you and some friends are deciding where to eat that night, you remember that conversation and choose the new restaurant based on your other friend's recommendation. The owner of the restaurant makes several hundred dollars from your table, and possibly many thousands of dollars in the coming years from you and your friends when you go back there—not as a result of *their* marketing, but as a result of an enthusiastic recommendation from your friend.

This is essentially the same thing you're doing when you email your list recommending a product or service as an affiliate. If you have been marketing to your list the right way, they'll see you as their trusted advisor. The only difference is, you will actually get paid (very well) for your recommendations.

How to Build a Strong Relationship with Your List and Make Maximum Profits

Here are a few guidelines I've picked up over the years, after writing and sending out literally thousands of emails to my list of now 700,000+ subscribers:

- **Never promote something *just* for the money.** Make sure it's actually a valuable program, or your subscribers will never trust you again.

- **Communicate as a real person;** never use an overly formal business tone in your email marketing, because it makes you sound like an impersonal company.

- **Mix it up with the media.** Put the occasional photo in your emails. Link to the odd video. Record some audio messages. Keep it interesting.

- **When people respond to your emails, respond back personally.** When your list gets too big, you won't be able to do this as you'll have too many responses coming in; but when you start out, you definitely should. On special occasions, you can do it even when you normally wouldn't or shouldn't. It's said that Steve Jobs occasionally took technical customer service calls at Apple in his later years.

- **Treat your subscribers as you want to be treated.** When you get a marketing email from someone, you can usually tell whether that person wants to help their subscribers, or only cares about making a quick buck. Your subscribers know you're a marketer, and that you want to make money. But show them you care (which I hope you genuinely do).

- **Get good at writing persuasive, benefit-rich email copy.** This comes with practice. When I first started writing emails to my newly built small list, my emails were terrible. But over time, my writing started to develop character, and I started to enjoy it.

- **Make *lots* of offers,** but do it in a cool way, while always providing value.

This list is a good summary of what you SHOULD do. Now, let's talk about what NOT to do.

What NOT To Do In Your Email Marketing

Here's how to burn out your list fast, so none of your subscribers will buy from you again:

- **Be inconsistent in your follow-up.** Email your subscribers daily for a few days; then don't email them for three months. Then suddenly start emailing them again.

- **Promote programs you know are crap**, and that you know your subscribers won't like—and will probably just refund.

- **Promote a new product every single day.**

- **Make sure that none of your emails offer any value to your subscribers.**

- **Never show appreciation for your subscribers.**

I get offered hundreds of thousands of dollars monthly by other trainers in my niche to promote their products and services. I turn them all down, mainly because I'm not that impressed with the quality of what they sell. Unless I really believe in something and would use it myself, I won't tell others to do the same. Another reason is, I prefer to promote MOBE programs, and make sure my affiliates get paid on every single sale made to people they refer to me.

Advantages of Level 2: You get to build a real asset, your own list. The value of that asset comes down to the size, and more importantly, the *responsiveness* of your list. Responsiveness is largely the result of the relationship you build with your subscribers. Do they see you as someone who offers value? As someone who they want to follow? As someone who cares about them? I've seen affiliate marketers with lists of fewer than 1,000 subscribers make more money than other affiliates with lists of over 50,000 subscribers!

Disadvantage: It's more work. You've got to write a lot of emails and create a lot more content. But once you've been doing it for a few months, it's really quite easy.

How to Increase Sales With Automated Email Follow-Up Sequences

Once someone subscribes to your list, it's important they hear from you immediately. If they don't, they'll forget you very fast; and then, when you do email them, they might not even recognize your name and think your email is spam. So it's a good idea to have an automated follow up sequence in place, ready to go. It might look something like this:

DAY 0: Send a welcome email to everyone who has opted into your list.

DAY 1: Send a new email making them an irresistible offer.

DAY 2: Remind those who haven't responded that they haven't ordered yet.

DAY 3: Send another quick, gentle reminder, highlighting your offer's benefits.

DAY 4: Remind those who still haven't responded about your offer, and possibly add a time sensitive "act now" second offer.

DAY5: Let your non-responders know that this is the last time they'll hear from you about this offer, and give them one last chance to get a great deal.

Note that this is just one example of a potential email follow-up process. If you don't want to sit down and write out 10 emails all at once, then just write one, and go get your first few email subscribers. As soon as they opt-in, they'll receive your **Day 0** email. Now you have 24 hours to write **Day 1**; and with that accountability weighing on you, you'll find it much easier to get it done. As long as that email is loaded into the email autoresponder before they reach the next day, it will go out on time. Then you'll have another 24 hours to write **Day 2**, and so on and so forth. I've used this method to write entire 30-day sequences before.

How to Build Your Own 'Money Getting' List

Building a list of email subscribers isn't that hard. My current list of over 700,000 subscribers started out with me generating my very first lead in early 2009, through placing ads on Google. The first thing you'll need is a lead capture page, also referred to as squeeze page or an opt-in page. It's just a one page website where a free gift is offered in exchange for someone's email address. The great part about the MOBE high ticket affiliate program, is that we actually give you a custom lead-capture page builder too. This means you can create endless lead capture pages yourself, even if you're like me and have no idea how to code or build websites. It's really easy to use—you just drag and drop the different parts of the page you want, change a few words, then click a few buttons—and your very own lead capture page is done! When you get access to it there will be short tutorial videos that walk you through the process.

Once it's built (which should take no more than 30 minutes), you then start placing ads to your lead capture page, instead of to an affiliate link for someone else's website. You get the person on your list, and then you have their permission to email them each day (or however often you want) with various offers using your affiliate links. The lead capture page saves that person's contact info to a database list, exclusive to you, that you can tap anytime you want.

Think of a lead capture page as a friendly bribe: *"Give me your email address, and I'll send you this free report..."* or *"Give me your email address, and I'll grant you access to this free video..."* or *"Give me your email address and phone number, and I'll give you a free one-on-one strategy session where we'll discuss..."*

or *"Give me all your contact information, and I'll personally introduce you to Chloë Moretz or Channing Tatum, your choice."*

The more of their contact details you ask for, the more you must offer in return. People will have no problem giving out their email for information they want - since most know they can easily unsubscribe at any time. But they'll be more protective of contact details like their phone number or physical mailing address; so you'll have to offer a lot more value for that information.

As a marketer, the more data you can collect, the more valuable the lead becomes. Just think about it; with an email address, phone number, and physical mailing address you have 3 channels to follow up with them. But when you're new, all you need to start building your list are email addresses. You can get their other details later on if you want to.

MOBE Case Study: The 'Masturbation Email' (And How It Cost Me A Car)

Words can be powerful things, and the words you use in your email marketing are no different. Use the right ones, and money flows in almost effortlessly. Use the wrong ones, and not only will people not buy, but it can get your email autoresponder account shut down!

I'm my own case in point here. Back in mid-2012, I was promoting another trainer's course, which was about Facebook marketing. It was selling for $497, and the commission was $220. It was marketed as a product launch, meaning that for several weeks, the anticipation and excitement for this product was built up, before it was put on sale for just seven days. I desperately wanted to win the contest they were holding for most affiliate sales. Why? Because the first prize was a $100,000+ Audi R8. I wanted to win it so badly that I put my entire business virtually on hold for a month.

D'oh! Looking back, that wasn't very smart. At the time, I was consistently generating $120,000+ in revenue per month—and in the month I was distracted promoting this product to my list for 4 weeks, my revenue plummeted to closer to $50,000 per month. That might not seem like such a bad thing to most people reading this, but by then I'd become accustomed to a certain income level.

I desperately wanted to get the most sales out of all the affiliates so I could win the car, so I was emailing (hammering) my list twice a day, telling them why they needed to buy. I had no problem doing that; the course was quite good, and I was actually one of its guest trainers. In the last 48 hours of the product launch, I found out that I was in Second Place. Out of thousands of affiliates, I was second in line to walk away with this car! Already I was asking the guy behind the launch how he was going to ship the car to Australia (where I then lived), and hinting to some of my family members I would soon have a new car pulling up in my driveway.

I was WAY ahead of the guy in Third place, and very close behind the person in First. I just needed to increase my total sales by about 10%, and I would win the car. So I decided that for those last 48 hours, I wasn't going to go home. I wouldn't sleep. My sole purpose in life would be to sell as many copies of this course to the people on my list.

So I started sending a lot more emails out to my list... and I started making insanely over-the-top bonus offers. *"Buy this course for $497, and I'll give you over $5,000 worth of my own courses, for free!"* I even offered people a free ticket to a live three-day training event I planned to host in San Diego a month later (and which I'd end up spending about $20,000 to put on) in an effort to get them to buy. The amount of value I was offering was ridiculous, and the sales came pouring in—but not fast enough. The guy coming First knew I was hot on his tail, so he was also promoting like crazy. I told myself, *"If only I could get more people on my list who were not opening the majority of my emails to actually open, they'd see my insane bonus offer and want to buy the course!"* What subject line could I possibly use, which would stand out among all the dozens of emails they received on a daily basis? What subject line would scream out for their attention, and create enough curiosity that they'd just have to open my email?

I know!

Masturbation.

I knew that would get really high open rates. How could someone resist opening it, just to see why the normally conservative tone of my emails had suddenly changed. Now, before you accuse me of sending dirty emails to my subscribers, I'll have you know the email itself wasn't one bit dirty—it was actually meant to make a point that people shouldn't procrastinate on buying the course. Here's the actual email:

SUBJECT: Masturbation

I love this line:

"Procrastination is like masturbation; In the end you're just screwing yourself."

(already I can see the hate mail coming in... lol)

But it's true. How often do you put something off till 'later'... and then never get it done.

Most people do this their ENTIRE lives.

Most people also end up financially struggling, and full of regrets.

As of now, there's 11 hours left for you to get Futuristic Marketing, before it's taken off the market.

You can put this off till 'later'... but, if you do, here's what you'll miss:

1. Futuristic Marketing: see everything you get here: www.futuristicmarketingbonus.com/bonuslink

2. The lead capture page software Jonathan's team paid a fortune to develop, that will do all the tech work for you

3. The automated webinar software (which my team will be setting up for you, as part of your bonus)

4. A private Facebook mastermind with me: if you ever get stuck, I'm only a message away.

5. My 45k bonus, which you can see here:
www.futuristicmarketingbonus.com/futuristic-marketing-bonus

You get EVERYTHING on that page. Yes... even the 17k 'done for you' set up, which we're offering to the first 300 new members only.

All I'll say is this:

The program gets my FULL endorsement. I believe if you get it... and you take it seriously... you'll look back on it as a key turning point in your online career.

You'll be GLAD I was so damn persistent about asking you to invest in it...

And, I'll be glad to hear about how your business is now churning along nicely.

Get it now, before it's too late:
www.futuristicmarketingbonus.com/bonuslink

As soon as you get it, email me at futuristicmarketingbonus@gmail.com, and, I'll make sure you get ALL the bonus's promised.

Talk soon,

Matt

I know, I know. It was still a highly inappropriate subject line to send out. But it worked. *Kind of.* That email got me one of the highest open rates I've ever experienced in over 7 years of sending emails. But it also got me some extremely high spam complaints. Apparently, some people were offended (can you believe it??)... and that got my email autoresponder account suspended for 2 weeks!

This happened at the worst possible time. With just 12 hours to go before the end of the product launch, and desperately needing more sales, I had no way of marketing to my list. I was dead in the water, and my dreams of racing my new Audi R8 down the highway slipped away from me. By the time the launch drew to a close, I was absolutely exhausted and defeated. I knew I'd lost. I went home and slept for over 14 hours straight.

Not only did I lose the car and halve my normal monthly revenue, but also I lost the ability to market to my list and another 2 weeks worth of revenue. The seven straight days of relentlessly promoting this course took its toll on my list. A lot of email marketers make this mistake on a regular basis, and burn out their list as a result.

It was a hard lesson to learn, something I'll never, ever do again. Learn from my mistake, so you never do something similar. Don't feel too sorry for me, though. In the end, I sold nearly 800 copies of that course and got paid $120 on each one.

How To Write Profit-Pulling Emails

Writing good emails is not that hard to do. In fact, anyone can write profit-pulling emails if they follow a few simple rules.

First, is subject matter. That's an easy one. You can write about:

- **Personal stories**
- **'How to' information**
- **Announcements**
- **Product reviews**
- **Opinion pieces**

At the back of this book in the appendix, I've put a bunch of some of my better emails promoting various products over the years. Feel free to model these if you want.

Once, at one of my MOBE affiliate training seminars (the Super Charge Summit), I was training attendees on how to write sales-producing emails from scratch in under 30 minutes. I challenged the audience to give me a topic to write about—any topic, even some inanimate object—and I would turn it into a promotion for one of my $49 courses. Someone pointed to a water jug on their table and challenged me to write about that. Someone else called out, *"Write about what you had for breakfast."* Then someone called out, and pointing above my head, said, *"Write about an air vent."* Now that sounded like a challenge! And within 30 minutes after getting off stage, I'd written this email:

> SUBJECT: How an Air Vent made me a small fortune…
>
> I'll never forget it.
>
> The year was 2008. I was a struggling university student, mowing lawns on the side of my university studies for 15 bucks / hour.
>
> One day while on my bed I was staring up at the ceiling, and looking at an air vent.
>
> I had one of those 'epiphany' moments.
>
> The air vent is part of a ventilation and air-conditioning system.
>
> In that system, there's a thermostat. If the temperature of the room increases past the set temperature, the thermostat turns the air conditioning on.
>
> If the temperate is too cold, it shuts the air conditioning off.
>
> The thermostat ensure the temperature remains within a certain temperature range.
>
> I realised in that moment that our own level of wealth works by a very similar system – only the 'thermostat' is our own mind set and comfort zone.
>
> When people with a poverty consciousness have extra money come into their lives, they find ways to subconsciously get rid of it (eg. they go spend it on more 'stuff' they don't need).
>
> When they are lacking money, they look a little bit harder for new ways to create wealth.
>
> Many people spend their entire lives stuck within a 'comfort zone' of wealth.

What I realised in that moment was that my own internal thermostat of wealth needed some serious adjustment.

I realised I was worth more than $15 / hour.

And in that moment, I got up off my bed, went to Google, and typed in 'make money online.'

That one little act dramatically altered the rest of my life.

And it all began with me innocently looking at an air vent!

Here's my promise to you:

If you make a decision right now to get started with MTTB and go through the 21 steps, and take the course seriously, it has the same potential to dramatically change YOUR life.

Many of the biggest shifts in wealth begin as small decisions and actions.

You have the decision to make right now – make the right one.

Get started now: www.mttbsystem.com/letter

As soon as you've done that, reply back to this email, and I'll give you the next step.

Speak soon,

YOUR NAME

I'll admit, it's not exactly a work of art... but it would still make sales if I sent it out to my list. If the story were true, maybe I would. With enough creativity, anything can be related back into a promotional email for just about any course, product, or service. It's just a matter of practice.

Even if you think you're a terrible writer, you can still write emails that make you a lot of money. Here's what I tell my own affiliates: write the way you speak. Write in a conversational tone. Imagine you're explaining the topic and offer to someone you care about; talk about how it's going to help them and why they should get it now. I recommend that instead of staring at a blank computer screen, you pick up your phone, find the voice recorder option, and talk out loud (*ideally when no one else is around*). Imagine you're telling someone you know about the product. You might start off with a story about how you used to have the problem that the product solves, then you got it, and then you're problem went away (if that's true). Then, being a good friend you recommend that they get it too. Or, you might share a case study (testimonial) of someone who used the product and got incredible results with it.

Once done, stop recording. Then play it back to yourself and transcribe what you said. Your tone will be more conversational, and that's exactly what you want in your emails. With enough practice, you won't even need to record your voice and transcribe - you'll just hear the inner conversational voice in your head and put the words onto the page (just like I'm doing right now).

One of our top Diamond affiliates is a 27 year old from London. He's one of the most enthusiastic guys I've ever met; when you're around him, you can't help but be happy. He writes just like he speaks. He doesn't bother much with capitalization or punctuation. His writing is all over the place, but full of value, not just from the information he gives and the offers he makes, but from the inspiration his bubbly prose gives. His subscribers love him; he's one of them made good, and he's incurably optimistic. When he recommends a product, he does it with conviction and not a hint of doubt that the person getting the email needs it. He earns an average of *well over $10,000 in sales* every time he sends a new email, with a good portion of that coming from his MOBE commissions (in total, he's done over $2.7 million with MOBE at the time of writing).

You don't need to be an expert on something in order to sell it. You don't even have to be a great writer. Often, you can just get the sales copy from the sales page (or the affiliate link you're promoting), and paraphrase from that. If you recommend a restaurant to a friend, you might not only talk about how good the food is, you might send them the link to the restaurant's website. And remember: *people will pay attention to you longer when you entertain them, not just educate them*. You'll notice in this book that I'm educating you—but I'm also entertaining you along the way, mainly through stories. This keeps it interesting and creates more of a bond. You can hear a voice or personality throughout my writing. Even though we've probably never met, you can get a sense for what I'd be like in person. If I've done my job right, then when we do meet one day at a live MOBE training event like the Titanium, Platinum, or Diamond Mastermind… you'll feel like we've met before.

You want to do the same thing in your writing to your own subscribers.

HTAM CASE STUDY

"Follow Up" Email Marketing Helps Retired Husband and Wife Team Earn $126,618.96, Build Nest Egg, and Travel

My name is Chris Beesley, and I live with my wife Susan outside London in the UK. To date, we've made $126,618.96 through the MOBE high ticket affiliate program. Our best single day was $15,850! We also qualified for the MOBE Motors program, where MOBE pays for our dream car, a BMW 3 series. (See details about MOBE Motors at: www.mobemotors.com)

Our main traffic method is Facebook, and we also do a good job of following up with leads. This has allowed us to make big money with small numbers. The fortune really is in the follow-up. Regularly emailing our subscribers and providing them with value is a crucial part of our success.

Before MOBE, we were accountants and management consultants working 6-7 days a week, 10-12 hours a day. In 2008, our pensions were wiped out and we started looking for another way to make money. We discovered MOBE and it has given us a new lease on life and a solution to our nest egg problem. We can now fulfill our passion – traveling, teaching, and training through a portable business model.

Chris & Susan Beesley (Diamond Members)

How To Get An Instant Influx Of Cash With Broadcast Emails

This is where you broadcast an email to everyone on your list, no matter where they are in your sequence. Whether they've just opted in yesterday or have been subscribed for over six months, they'll get your email. The advantage of broadcasts is they're a lot more organic than most emails. You can tie them to local events (a holiday, something going on in the news, etc.) that's already on the minds of your subscribers, so open rates are usually higher.

The disadvantage is that if you rely only on live broadcast messages, and you happen to forget to send the email, you just lost a chance to bring in potential revenue. Maybe you're traveling, or you just completely forgot to write one, but every time you fail to send one, you've missed an opportunity to build a relationship with and monetize your list.

So which is better, automated sequences or live email broadcasts? A combination of both, actually. I have a 30-day, well-optimized email sequence that my new leads (and the leads the MOBE affiliates send me) automatically go into. I've made each email the very best it can be—because I know that my best chance to monetize the lead is when they're still new. Then, once a day, I send a live broadcast email to everyone who has already been through my 30-day sequence.

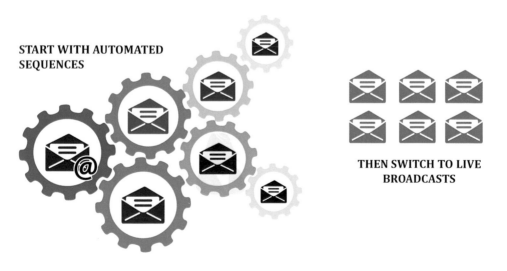

START WITH AUTOMATED SEQUENCES

THEN SWITCH TO LIVE BROADCASTS

How do you do that? With segmentation. Speaking of which...

How To Double Sales With Segmentation [Advanced]

I'm a little hesitant to discuss this technique, because I can imagine some of you cringing about "how technical this all sounds" and then being tempted to use that as an excuse to do nothing. So let me just give you the basics, and tell you that there are affiliate marketers who make hundreds of thousands of dollars per year who never segment. But if you do segment your list and talk to each segment differently, you can easily extract twice as much money out of that list.

Sometimes I'll segment based on geography. As I write this, I'm about to host an enormous training event for our MOBE affiliates in Sydney. It's rare that we do one of these types of events, so it's a big deal. Rather than promoting it to my entire list—which is made up of a majority of people who live outside Australia—I segmented it based on the country the subscribers live in. Obviously, anyone living in Australia will get emails about it. People living in nearby New Zealand will get a few, too. People living in Sydney itself will get a lot. Granted, it's more work to do this, but not that much more. Most mainstream autoresponders let you do it with a few clicks of your mouse.

Other times, I'll segment on a previous action (or lack thereof). Every time I send out a broadcast email to my hundreds of thousands of subscribers, I know the majority aren't going to open it. This may be for a number of reasons. Maybe they've changed their email address. Maybe they don't see the email. Maybe they're not interested anymore. Maybe the email wasn't delivered, due to ISP blocking (ISPs are like the police of the email highways, and occasionally block things). Maybe the email *does* get delivered, but ends up in the spam folder, and my subscriber never even sees it. There are many reasons my email may not be opened.

If you go into your email inbox and look at the emails you get from different businesses, and then search for emails from only one of them, I'll bet you find you don't read every single one. On average, only a third of my subscribers might open an email. If I've spent an hour crafting the perfect email message, that annoys me. I want them all to see it. So instead of writing a new email the next day to send out and hope this is the one that gets their attention, I send the same email out to everyone who didn't open it, changing just the subject line.

For all they know, this second email is an entirely new one! Again, most autoresponders make this easy.

Sometimes I'll segment based on time on the list. If I only want to email leads who have been on my list for 30 days or more (e.g., leads that aren't still within my 30-day follow-up sequence), then I just take the current date, subtract 30 days, and search for the segment of people who have been on my list since before then. Then I email them specifically.

Why Getting Good at Conversions Will "Extract" Money From Your List

At my very first live event in March 2012, "Online Income Revolution," I did a live demo from the stage to make a point. I wanted to teach the 46 people in that room, who had each paid $1,000 to be there, what building a fast-growing and scalable business was all about. So I told them bluntly, "The speed at which you scale will largely depend on how quickly you're able to extract money from a list of subscribers, and then reinvest it back into acquiring more subscribers, so you can do the same thing over and over in ever-increasing amounts."

Does that sound a bit ruthless to you—this idea of "extracting" money from a group of people in the shortest amount of time possible? I don't mean it in a ruthless way; in fact, quite the opposite. People aren't going to buy from you unless they really want what you offer, and they'll never come back to buy again if that first transaction isn't a pleasant experience. Over 90% of all the money MOBE has made has come from people we've sold to before. Another way of saying that is… of our first $100 million in revenue, $90 million came from our *previously* existing customers. Isn't that amazing? Yet you would be shocked at how many people ignore that obvious source of income!

If you're not capturing the contact details of your customers at the point of sale, so you can follow up and make repeat offers to them, then you're leaving serious money on the table. I would estimate that you're reaping less than one-third of your potential rewards (and I'm being conservative with that figure). In other words, businesses that aren't following up and offering more expensive, more valuable programs on the "back end" are making their job three times harder than it needs to be.

In any industry, the businesses that extract the most money from their customers while providing them with the most value will win. This total amount of money is referred to as the "Lifetime Customer Value," or LCV. If you and I are competing against each other to acquire the same customers, and your average customer spends $500 with you over their lifetime while mine only spends $250 with me, then you've got an enormous advantage over me. In fact, you can afford to spend double what I can to acquire a customer. If the average cost of acquiring a customer in our industry is $200, you're going to make a $300 profit on each sale ($500 LCV - $200 cost = $300 profit). I, on the other hand, will only make $50 per sale ($250 LCV - $200 cost = $50 profit).

What happens if more competitors enter our market and start competing for the same customers? They're going to start placing ads too. The demand for ad media goes up, but the supply is relatively fixed. So prices go up (*maybe you remember this from those economics classes you took back in college*). Let's say that the new cost to acquire a customer rises to $300. Now I'm in trouble! You can still afford to buy customers and make a $200 profit; I, on the other hand, am out of business. Buying customers for $300 that are worth only $250 to me means I'm losing money on every transaction. If I keep advertising at those rates, I'll burn through all my cash and be out of business.

This is how all industries work—and the one guarantee I can give you is that if there's money to be made in a market, the amount of competition will only go up over time. *So maximizing average customer lifetime value needs to be a major focus for you.*

One of the things I'm always thinking about is, *"How do I come up with more valuable (and more expensive) programs that my customers will want to buy?"* The great thing about selling to existing customers is that it's pretty much FREE from a marketing standpoint. You don't have to spend any more money to acquire them—you already did that with the first sale. That's why for the average business, the greatest untapped gold mine is their own customer list, and it's hiding in plain sight!

If you're not capturing the contact details of your customers at the point of sale, so you can follow up and make repeat offers to them, then you're leaving serious money on the table.

Recently, I came up with a $60,000 accountability program, and I offered it only to my very best clients, those who had spent a minimum of $56,000 with me already. I offered it on stage at a very high-end training event in Cancun, Mexico, to about 50 people in the room. I sold three of these program on the spot. One of them backed out, but 2 moved forward. An instant $120,000. For their investment, they get direct access to me on Skype *every day for a year*, where they can ask me questions and get help with their business. Keep in mind that I charge (and get) $5,000 an hour for one-on-one consulting, so with the amount of time they get over a year, they're getting me cheap! And I give them homework that they *have* to do. The rule is, if they miss three days in row, they get kicked out of the program with no refund. This keeps them accountable—and so far, both are doing really well.

I'm currently working on a $250,000 one-year mentoring program, where MOBE affiliates can come live and work out of the same building I operate out of in Kuala Lumpur. They'll get full access to the MOBE Film Studio (where I make almost all my marketing videos), and their own private penthouse office

MOBE Film Studio Kuala Lumpur

with one of the best views of the city center available. Sweet! Each day, they'll have very clear tasks to accomplish in their business, tasks I'll be overseeing. Results will be literally guaranteed—and this will only be for people willing to invest a year of their life, and work harder than they've ever worked to generate $1 million in commissions. The application process to get one of these four (and only four) coveted positions will be long and arduous—but it needs to be that way, to make sure only the right people get in. I don't want to spend a year trying to coach someone who doesn't take action.

Once I release this program, I have no doubt that it will sell out fast. And yes, there will be an *enormous* commission to any affiliate (it could be you!) who brings me a leads who buys one of these $250,000 programs.

I'm telling you these things, because these are a small sample of what I offer on the back-end to give my clients more value, and make the majority of my profits.

In your own business, building out and strengthening your back-end needs to become your focus once the front-end customer acquisition process is dialed in. That's where you'll make the *really* big money. Remember there are few problems in business that can't be solved by making more sales. Now you may hearing all this and thinking, "but Matt, I don't want to create my own high-ticket programs and sell them to my customers - I wouldn't know what program to create, and wouldn't want to do all the work fulfilling them."

Here's the good news for you as an affiliate marketer; you don't have to create back-end programs. You don't have to do all that extra work. The MOBE high ticket affiliate program already has all that in place *for you*. And here's the bad news: if you join any other affiliate program besides MOBE, you likely won't get paid a cent on the back end. You will only get paid measly commissions on their front end products (which sell for a few hundred bucks or less), while they make the real money selling expensive programs on the back end to the customers YOU brought them! You won't even know this is happening unless the customer tells you. That's how 99.9% of all affiliate programs in the world (besides MOBE) operate.

Having been an affiliate marketer for several years myself, I know what it's like to put your time and energy into generating traffic so you can generate commissions. So I decided that when I created the MOBE high ticket affiliate program back in 2011, I was going to pay affiliates on the back end. You bring me a customer, and I'll make sure you get paid on whatever MOBE sells to that customer for the rest of their lives. Seriously, the rest of their lives. That means that if you sell a $10 MOBE e-book to a customer and two years later they attend a live event and they buy something—you'll get paid on that sale, even if the commission is $10,000.

We use a sophisticated affiliate tracking program to track all of this that ensures you get paid on every transaction. That's what our affiliates love about

> *Building out and strengthening your back-end needs to become your focus once the front-end customer acquisition process is dialed in.*

us, and why they're so loyal. We've made paying our affiliates the most money possible a major focus in the company, and they can see that.

Once again, here are the steps to making money in affiliate marketing:

* **Find a great affiliate program to promote.** Hands down, the greatest is MOBE.

* **Learn how to consistently generate both quantity and quality of clicks** to your affiliate links, each and every day.

* **Focus on one traffic method**, and don't try learning more until you're getting consistent results with just one.

* **Once you're making steady sales as a result, start to build your own list**.

Even More Ways You Can Extract Money from a List

Once you've got a nice list built, you can start doing other activities besides sending emails to promote your offers. You can host teleconferences and webinars (using services like GoToWebinar.com), where you can sell programs that earn you thousands of dollars per hour. The first time I did this, I had 14 people on a live call, and nervously read through a script I'd got from listening to someone else's webinar. At the end, I got one sale for $1,697 (my commission on that as an affiliate was $1,000). It was like Christmas! There's no better feeling in the world than discovering you really can create money almost out of thin air.

I can tell you about things like this all day—but until you experience it, you won't fully appreciate how good it feels. That's why I keep telling you to TAKE ACTION. Don't be one of these people who read this book and then never do anything with the information. At some of my more advanced seminar trainings like the Diamond Mastermind, we actually teach people how to host their own sales webinars, and have them host their first one that same night. It gets the students outside of their comfort zone, but at the end they feel very good about having done it.

All these things I'm telling you will help you monetize your list more effectively. As you're building your list, nothing is more important. You finance the growth of that list (i.e. placing paid ads to get new subscribers) through the commissions you make promoting to your current subscribers.

To really drive this point home… at a seminar I hosted once, I remember standing on stage, picking up a knife, and slicing a lemon in half. On the table in front of me were two glasses. Holding one lemon-half above the first glass, I gave it a gentle squeeze and a few measly drops came out. *"This is most of you,"* I told them. *"The lemon is your list, and the juice coming out of it is money. Most of you are lucky to get a few drops out of it, if any at all."*

I then picked up the other half, and said, *"And this is my business."* I gave it a firm squeeze and juice poured out, half filling the glass. *"See the difference?"*

Most new Level 2 marketers are lucky if they extract a few commissions from their lists. When it comes to promoting, you've got to be a lot more proactive than this. Sending out a few emails a week with lukewarm offers won't cut it. You need to send *daily* emails and be unafraid to tell people to buy, because you believe in the product and think they can benefit from it.

If you're not getting that much juice out of your list, don't blame your list. A lot of new affiliate marketers do. And they'll say things like, *"They just don't have the money."* But that's not true. It's not that they don't have the money; they just don't have the money for you. So if you're not making sales, ask yourself, *"how do I improve my own marketing skills,"* rather than automatically blaming the people on your list.

By the way, if reading about "extracting" money from a list, and "squeezing the juice" out of them is making you feel uneasy, then again, let me stress: This isn't about taking people's money when they don't want to buy, or fooling them in any way. I assume you're promoting items that you, as an affiliate, actually believe in. This is crucial! I've never recommended something to my audience that I didn't think would genuinely help them. That's why I turn down most joint venture offers.

I could make millions of dollars of extra money each year if I promoted the latest fad or craze or product launch. It would be easy money. But I won't. Neither should you.

So, does all this talk about sending email to "warm traffic" sound like a lot of work? If so, remember, Level 2 is optional. I advise that you get here eventually, so you can build your own list from which you can create income-on-demand at any time. However, you can still make great money remaining at Level 1, if you just focus on getting good at generating traffic.

The MOBE High Ticket Affiliate Program is the world's best HTAM system that pays you up to $13,500 per sale!

Backend high-ticket sales are made FOR YOU: MOBE does the work and deposits commissions directly into your bank account twice a month!

PLUS ... you get a **personal coach** that will walk you through a simple 21-step training program on how to make your first BIG commission (even if you have zero computer skills!)

90% of the work required to run a business is Done For You:

✓ No products to create
✓ No fulfillment or customer service
✓ No payment processing
✓ No website design or hosting
✓ No sales presentations or funnels to create
✓ No selling in person or over the phone

... It's all Done For You!

Join today at: www.fivefigureaffiliatemarketing.com

CHAPTER EIGHT

Level 3: Creating Your Own Products and Sales Funnels

O nce you've gotten really good at Levels 1 and 2—and I do mean *really good*, because if you aren't, you're going to fail miserably if you try this—you can start creating your own unique products, and sell them instead of (or alongside) the products you promote as an affiliate. You don't even have to be my competitor. The MOBE Marketplace is growing by leaps and bounds, and I allow other Level 3 marketers to play in my world, **if and only if** their products are high-quality and offer substantial commissions.

The big advantage of this stage is **positioning**. When you have your own websites, sales funnels, fancy videos, and products, now you really are the guru and the expert in the eyes of your audience.

Videos, websites, sales funnels, products—all these are what I call "positioning devices." When done well, they establish you as an expert and authority in your niche. They make you stand out above the competition, and that's crucial in any field. Pretend for a moment you were faced with needing a life-saving surgery. You had 2 surgeons to choose from: one who had a famous TV show, or one you had never heard of. You would likely go with the one on TV—even though he may not be a better surgeon and may cost a lot more! Why? Because you want the best, and if someone is on TV with their own show (*the show is the positioning device*) that carries a lot of credibility. *That* is the power of positioning.

Being a Level 3 marketer is a career decision, and it takes a lot of hard work and the right personality. But if you decide it's for you (and accomplish it), you can easily make 7 figures per year (or more).

In this chapter, you'll learn:

* **How My Most Terrifying Moment on Stage Led To Over $1 Million In Sales**

* **How to Create Your First Product...** and how to hire a copywriter to sell it

* **What Gets Measured Gets Improved:** Why it's important to track your numbers and set goals to beat your previous records

Let's get started...

How My Most Terrifying Moment On Stage Led To Over $1 Million In Sales

The first time I ever spoke on stage at a live marketing event (which also happened to be one of the most terrifying moments of my life), I was teaching Facebook marketing. The truth is, I wasn't even that great at it. Don't get me wrong; I was generating a few hundred dollars a day and knew the basics well, but there were other people who knew a lot more than me. After the seminar was over, I made sure to get a video recording of that speech and posted it on YouTube and Facebook. When people saw me in that video, teaching a few hundred people at a big Internet marketing seminar, their opinion of me changed *instantly*. All of a sudden, I became "the Facebook marketing guru." After all, I was on stage teaching others about this topic and they had seen the video proof; I must be a Facebook marketing guru, right? That's how most people's minds work. They see someone teaching on a topic and automatically view that person as an authority on the topic (whether it's deserved or not). In my case, it was; and suddenly a lot more people wanted to buy what I was selling.

I leveraged the hell out of that recording, for over 12 months straight! That 90-minute video (which you can see for yourself at **www.MOBE.com/**

thetruthabouttraffic) easily made me **over $1 million** in the coming years, just from the extra credibility it gave me. That's the power of having a good positioning device. Ideally, you want many.

Having your own products, speaking on stages, getting fancy videos made about you… you should only do all of this *after* you've made some good money at Level 1 and 2. If you're starting out in affiliate marketing, don't worry about creating positioning devices just yet. Learn how to get clicks first, and make some commissions. Once you've made some commissions, start building your list. Once you've made a few hundred thousand dollars, then consider creating your own products.

Quite a few of the very top earners within the MOBE high ticket affiliate program are at Level 3. Despite what a lot of people mistakingly think, these top earners don't promote MOBE products first. They promote *themselves* first, and then they sell MOBE products on the back end. For example, one of our Diamond affiliates, Michelle Pescosolido, positions herself as "The Facebook Expert." She talks about building your business on Facebook, and targets owners in the home business niche. They buy her and her brand first. Then she promotes her own programs, along with MOBE's.

How To Create Your First Product

I'll use creating a product from a live event as an example, since it's the one I'm most familiar with. My very first "real" product was an eight-module video training program that taught Internet marketers how to monetize an email list. I'd been doing email marketing for a couple years then, and I was pretty good at it. The only reason I got that training program done, though, was because I committed to it big-time—just as the only reason I was able to complete this book so fast was because I committed to writing the entire first draft over one weekend, and told my entire email list (over 700,000 people) that I was going to do it. It really helps when you have a solid deadline, some external accountability, and also when you put yourself in a new environment (like me locking myself up in a hotel room seven minutes away from where I live with no Internet).

With my HTAM system, 90% of the work required to run a business is Done For You
(we take care of fulfillment, payments, websites, sales funnels, and more).
Go to **www.fivefigureaffiliatemarketing.com** to get paid up to $13,500 on high-ticket sales
made for you!

It will be hard to create your first product; I won't lie to you. But once you do it, you will feel a major sense of accomplishment, because you'll have done something that very few people ever do.

After creating the product, you need a copywriter to write the words used to sell the product on a sales page. Most copywriters who think they're good are actually not, and most who try to charge you ridiculous prices (which is just about all of them) aren't worth it. Don't get me wrong here, though. A truly good copywriter is worth their weight in gold. I've spent *many* hundreds of thousands of dollars over the last few years on copywriters like that. And made tens of millions of dollars with their copy.

I'll give you one tip, though: if you can push a copywriter around too easily on their prices, that's not a good sign. The best copywriters know how good they are, are often booked up for months in advance, and are always willing to walk if you won't meet their price. The copywriters who churn out sales letters for $50 are a dime a dozen, and their copy is not even worth what you paid them. Stay away from them.

How much should you pay a copywriter? It depends on the deal. Usually, I'll pay a fixed amount per job. Anywhere from $1,000 to $5,000 is within the ballpark, although I've paid more. If you're going to hire a copywriter, this is one part of your business you shouldn't approach with a frugal mindset. You should hire the best copywriter you can afford. All good copywriters will have a portfolio of work to show you, and references you can check.

Unfortunately, being able to recognize whether a copywriter can write good copy or not requires you to know what good copy looks like. This is something that only comes through experience. If a copywriter shows you that they've written copy for some big names in your industry, don't be impressed just yet. Ask them how many letters they've done for that big name, and to see some of them. If they can only show you one, then you know they weren't good enough to get asked back. If they worked for the same guy for years (and that person is a successful marketer), think seriously about hiring them yourself.

Why Watching Your Numbers Guarantees Improvement

In my office, I have a huge TV screen that sits right in front of my desk. On it, is an enormous online dashboard, which shows me all my key metrics. It's so big (and right in front of me) that I can't help but look at it constantly throughout the day. This constant measurement keeps me focused and on track. I first started obsessing over numbers back in 2011, when I noticed my income one month was about $3,700, and decided I was going to beat it the next month. I did. And then the next month, I put all my focus into beating the previous month's income. And I did. Till this day, the desire to beat my previous record month is what drives me.

I've used this method in other areas of my life too. For a long time, I wanted to lose weight and get fit. I was never obese or anything- but I wanted to take care of myself. No matter how many times I tried to eat healthy and work out each day though, I just couldn't stick with it.

So I decided to start recording my weight. Every day, I would write down the date and my weight, then plot a simple line graph so I could see the trend. I still do this, and on any given day, I know exactly what I weigh. And because this number is in my conscious mind, it influences my choices throughout the day. When I'm offered dessert at dinner, a little voice in the back of my mind reminds me my weight has been trending up in the last few days, so I reply with a "No thanks." When I'm feeling lazy at 7 PM (my usual work-out time) and don't want to run and work up a sweat, the excuses start. Again, that little voice appears. It says, "stop making excuses you fat bastard, your weight's been on an upward trend and you're getting too far into the 80 kilograms range - get on that treadmill!" Ok, it doesn't say that, exactly. It's more like, "You've got a lot to do tonight. There's not enough time to work out." But because I'm focused on my weight, the excuse-making self-sabotaging voice is silenced. At MOBE events, it's always amusing when people come up to me and tell me how much weight I've lost compared to the version of me they saw in my older marketing videos.

If you want to improve any part of your life—business, relationships, health, literally anything—here's the secret: measure it and observe the numbers daily. The mere act of measurement and paying attention to the numbers (and how they're trending) will influence you to naturally want to improve them. It's almost like a built-in mechanism.

So with that said, what numbers should you focus on in your business?

The first is cash. How much cash did your business bring in today? How much cash did it send out? I look at this *daily.* This was a habit I learned the hard way, when after 6 months of not watching my cash flow, I realized I was bringing in huge sums of revenue, but it was flowing out in expenses just as fast.

The next thing I look at is how much cash my business has brought in for the month so far, and what it's projected to do (at the current average daily rate) by the end of the month. Let's say it's the 5th of the month, and your affiliate business has made $250 in sales so far. Next, work out your average daily amount of cash, which is $50 per day ($250 / 5 days = $50 /day). On average, there's roughly 30.5 days in a month. So multiply the days in the month by the average daily sales you're making: 30.5 x $50 = $1,525. That shows you're on track to do a tidy $1,525 this month, or $18,300 in the coming 12 months.

The next thing to do is look at your previous best-month record. Let's say it was $900, and you want to see how the current month is stacking up. $1,525 - $900 = $625. According to this projection, you'll beat your previous record month by $625 if you keep making $50 a day. Expressed as a percentage, you'll exceed it by 69.5% ($625 / $900 = 0.695).

So you're on track to have a very good month. Month-to-month growth of 69.5% is amazing. That's why every single month, your overriding mindset must be, *"I need to beat my previous monthly revenue number."* That is what has been driving me since late 2011 ever since I started trying to beat my previous records. In my business, my biggest and most challenging competitor is myself. I focus on bettering my personal best. I highly recommend you do the same.

Now if you don't have fancy online dashboards like I have, don't worry. Just use pen and paper to work it out each day, like I did when starting out.

Each day, write your numbers down on a sticky note and put it to the side of your computer screen. This will keep you focused.

"But Matt, what if I've made $0 so far this month?"

Well, the good news is that you have a really low target to beat next month! I say that only half-jokingly. If your previous monthly record is $0, then you only have to make one commission next month to beat your record. So each day ask yourself, "What can I do to bring in a sale? What can I do *right now* to increase that number up from $0?" Then go and do that immediately.

When you force yourself to think this way, you won't get distracted by shiny objects, or waste time on non-income producing activities (like getting pretty business cards made up). You will focus only on cash-generating activities.

Remember: until a sale is made, until you acquire your first customer, you don't have a real business.

Starting a business is NOT about fancy logos, websites, and mission statements. Starting a business is about doing whatever is necessary to bring in sales right now. You need to focus on getting the cash coming in. Without it, you can't fund the growth of your business. You can't pay for traffic. You can't pay yourself... and you won't get any positive reinforcement that the time you're investing is paying off. The beautiful thing about making sales every day is that you're constantly getting positive reinforcement—and it's a huge motivator.

Another key metric you want to focus on is daily traffic. How many clicks did your affiliate links get today? How many leads did you generate? A good affiliate program like MOBE's will give you all these numbers when you login to your stats back office.

And of course, a really important number to watch is your ROI numbers on each traffic source. In my own business, I watch this daily. Let's say I spend $200 on an ad source. After a week, I may still be in the red. I've outlaid $200 and don't have a single sale yet. But as that traffic goes through my marketing process (i.e.. they get my email marketing and other follow ups), the buyers will inevitably surface. That -$200 loss may turn into +$800 profit after the first 30 days (a positive ROI of 400%). Usually, I want to see a positive ROI after 90 days. If I can get one faster, that's even better. Every day, someone on my team updates me on all the numbers and presents them in a neatly organized report. I gloss over them, looking for trends and red flags. If something is wrong, the numbers will tell you fairly quickly.

By the way, if you're reading all this and thinking, *"but I'm not a numbers person!,"* then you either need to *find* one, or, bring someone onto your team who *is* one.

CHAPTER NINE

Building Your Business

O nce you've established yourself as an affiliate marketer and have the basics down cold, you need to get serious about building your business. This process is especially important when you step up to Level 2, if you choose to do so. However, many of the topics I'll discuss in this chapter apply just as readily to an affiliate marketing business at any stage. So I advise against skipping any of the sections in this chapter, because you might find them useful whether you're at Level 1, 2, or 3.

In this chapter, you'll learn:

* **How To Make Millions of Dollars When Most People Don't Want What You're Selling**

* **The Importance of Building Your Own Email List...** And 5 More Ways To Monetize It

* **Poor Email, Rich Email (A Case Study)**

* **How To Generate Sales With Facebook Groups:** A simple, free strategy that gets massive results

* **Facebook Fan Pages vs Facebook Groups:** Which Is Better?

* **How To Get Better Results By Single-Tasking**

* **The Insider Rules To Making Money Online**

* **The Dangers of 'Learned Helplessness'**

* **Financial Freedom & The Mediocre Masses**

As you build your business, your email list will become a valuable asset. Monetize it by promoting the offers in my HTAM system, which pays you up to $13,500 per sale. Sign up at **www.fivefigureaffiliatemarketing.com.**

Let's get started…

How To Make Millions of Dollars When Most People Don't Want What You're Selling

Let's face it, most people aren't going to buy from you. In fact, over 95% of all the clicks you generate will not result in sales. For most affiliate marketers, less than 1 out of 300 of the clicks they generate will be from a person who ends up pulling out a credit card and buying.

Does that sound like a low number to you?

Maybe it is. But even if only one out of 300 clicks results in a sale, you can still make a fortune on those numbers. I've made many tens of millions of dollars off numbers like that. You see, it all comes down to the *economics* of your business. How much do you need to spend to acquire a customer, and what's the average customer worth to you over their lifetime—i.e. how much do they spend with your business? If you buy 300 clicks at $1 each, for a total of $300, and it gets you just one customer, then you've just bought a customer for $300. If your average customer spends $600 with you, then you can and *should* keep buying customers at those prices since you're making $300 profit on each one.

Another way of looking at this is… for every $1 you invest, you get back $2. If there was a slot machine in Las Vegas that paid out a guaranteed $2 for every $1 you fed into it, you would play at it all day (and night) long. That's what business is fundamentally about: being able to buy customers profitably.

The Importance of Building Your Own Email List (And 5 More Ways To Monetize It)

If you've spent any amount of time learning about marketing (and particularly direct response marketing) then you've heard this old chestnut: *"The money's in the list."*

I remember the first time MOBE crossed $5 million in revenue in a single month. I also remember looking at the number of active email leads I had on the list that I was marketing to each and every month. I calculated that for every lead on my list, they'd spent, on average, around $8 with me that month. That's pretty good; I know a lot of marketers who do less than half of that. The month before that, the numbers were very similar. But in my best months, the average lead on my list has spent a lot more.

As a very broad average, the typical email lead on your list is going to spend between $2-$3 per month with you. And that's assuming you do a good job following up, sending them emails regularly (ideally daily) about programs with irresistible offers that they're interested in. As you get better at following up and getting conversions, you can expect to make a lot more per lead. The reason why MOBE generates higher amounts of revenue per subscriber comes down to a few main factors:

1. **Our marketing is better.** We know what our subscribers want, and we present our offers with hard-hitting, seductive sales copy and authenticity, so they're as irresistible as they can be. The big advantage I have is that I once was my average customer. I was that struggling new business owner, making no money, overworked and underpaid. I spent years being that person. So when I'm putting new marketing together, I can put myself in the shoes of my prospects and have a good idea of what they're thinking, what they want, and how they'll respond.

2. **We use multiple media to engage our subscribers.** Our main channels are email, Facebook, webinars, phone, direct mail, and live events. But we use many others as well. Many online businesses rely on email too much.

3. **We offer much more expensive and valuable programs than our competitors.** Every day, we sell $10,000 programs, $17,000 programs, and $30,000 programs. During special promotions, we sell the odd $60,000 program. So far, the record for the highest single transaction is $120,000. These programs cost a lot more time and money to fulfill, and it has taken us several years to create programs that are worth those kind of prices. But when your business is able to offer programs like this, it doesn't take many sales to start averaging $100,000+ days.

As you build your business, your email list will become a valuable asset. Monetize it by promoting the offers in my HTAM system, which pays you up to $13,500 per sale. Sign up at **www.fivefigureaffiliatemarketing.com**.

4. **Most people seriously overestimate how many customers they need to make a lot of money.** It's not about going wide; it's about going deep. Instead of thinking you need thousands of customers to make millions of dollars (a wide reach), you actually only need a few hundred really good customers *if* you market high-priced, high-value programs and follow up really well (you go deep). My highest-paying 100 customers have *easily* spent more than the bottom lowest paying 10,000 customers combined!

The first thing most new marketers do wrong is they 'sell from their heels.' Legendary copywriter Gary Halbert used to talk about this, and how a lot of entrepreneurs are afraid to sell, so they do it with fear, hesitation, and as an afterthought, at the last moment in their interaction with a potential buyer. Don't be this person. You want to be *unafraid* to sell. You want to do it with confidence and conviction. If you don't believe in what you're promoting, then you shouldn't be promoting it in the first place.

When I look at the top affiliates in MOBE, those who make the lion's share of the money, the one thing they have in common is that they're not afraid to promote. Some were at first, but they soon got over it. So when someone joins your list and you're sending them a promotional email, don't be afraid to promote hard.

Poor Email, Rich Email (A Case Study)

Here are two emails I could send to a new subscriber on my list. Read them both, and then choose which one you think would motivate more subscribers to buy. One email is written by someone who clearly lacks belief in their own value, who is afraid to sell, and who is more worried about not offending anyone than making a sale. The other is written by someone who is ready to make sales now, and communicates with confidence and authority. Both promote a MOBE course called Traffic Masters Academy.

Here's Email #1:

> **SUBJECT:** Thank you for subscribing to get my emails.
>
> Hi, my name is Matt. Thanks for joining my email list, which you just subscribed to.
>
> I really appreciate it, and I'm going to do my very best to give you a lot of value so you want to stay subscribed for the long term. If at any time you feel I email you too much, you can unsubscribe. Over the next 10 days, I'm going to send you an email each day where I'll explain some basics about generating leads. I'm quite new to this, so I'm not yet by any means an expert - but I am learning. I also promote a program which talks more about this which you can get from me (but don't worry, you don't have to buy it if you don't want to).
>
> Keep an eye out for tomorrow's email, where I'll explain to you three things that most people do wrong when it comes to getting leads.
>
> Thanks for reading.
>
> Matt

Now check out Email #2, by an affiliate who is here to offer value through selling valuable programs—and is therefore unafraid to tell someone they should buy.

> **SUBJECT:** Welcome to my list (and how to start generating your first few leads in the next 2 hours).
>
> Right off the bat, I'm going to tell you that the emails you get from me are going to be different. I'm not going to beat around the bush. You joined my list for a reason; you want to learn how to start generating traffic and leads right now.
>
> You understand that without a consistent daily lead flow in your business, you have no business.
>
> So let me tell you what you need to do next, if you're ready to immediately start getting more leads in your business and you're the kind of person who knows the importance of taking action immediately.

As you build your business, your email list will become a valuable asset. Monetize it by promoting the offers in my HTAM system, which pays you up to $13,500 per sale. Sign up at **www.fivefigureaffiliatemarketing.com**.

First of all, if you want to learn how to generate traffic, you should only take advice from those who are generating large sums of traffic today. What worked a year ago does not necessarily work now.

Step 1) The most comprehensive course on how to start generating leads immediately is called Traffic Masters Academy. It's a course created by some of the highest affiliate marketers in the industry, who have collectively made millions of dollars from their traffic campaigns; they know what they're doing, and can show you how to do the same.

Step 2) Once you get this course (which I suggest you do right now), forward your email receipt to me. Just send it to this same email address I'm sending you this from. As a fast-action bonus when you do this in the next 24 hours, I'm going to offer you 30 minutes of my time (valued at over $397 per hour) where I'll show you how to get started.

I'll also give you my top five performing ads of all time. You'll be able to swipe and deploy these in your own marketing and watch the leads roll in.

If you're ready to start generating more leads right now, then get this course now: **TrafficMastersAcademy.com**.

Talk soon,

Matt

So, who are you going to buy from? The second writer is a lot more compelling in getting the reader to act. They don't ask you or suggest you get the course; they tell you to get the course. They write as if they know this is the single greatest answer to all your traffic problems.

You may be thinking, *"Well, that's all right for you, Matt—you know how to write email copy that brings in sales. But what if I can't write very well?"*

Well, if you're a MOBE affiliate, then you don't need to be that great at writing! We give you email "swipe" copy (as we call it in the industry) that you can copy, paste, and send to your list. I recommend you tweak the emails a little so they have some of your personality in them, but 90% of the writing is already done for you.

Over time, you'll get good at writing emails. It's just a matter of practice.

How To Generate Sales With Facebook Groups: A Free Strategy That Gets Massive Results

Added all up, this simple, free strategy has made me millions of dollars. You'll probably be tempted to write it off as being way too simple to work—but trust me, it does!

When I first started doing email marketing back in 2009, I would send an email to my list (then just a couple hundred people) and see open rates of close to 30%! Wow—almost a third of my subscribers were opening my emails. That was pretty impressive to me. These days, I'm lucky if I get 5% open rates. But then again, my email list has over 700,000 people on it, and many of those subscribers have been there for years, changed email addresses, lost interest, etc.

Low open rates on an aged list is perfectly normal. But across the industry, open rates are much lower than they used to be. There was once a time when getting an email was an occasion for excitement, and you opened every single one—remember? Then it became the new normal, and eventually spammers ruined it for the rest of us. Nowadays, as I was recently reminded by a cynical cartoon, it's the other way around—we love getting real mail (especially checks!). Today, getting another email is a nuisance. People get way too many, and they're in a sorting/deleting mindset when scrolling through their inbox. Plus, a lot of their attention has gone to other media.

Like Facebook.

Let's get serious here…

HTAM CASE STUDY

Feza Sengul Finds Success Promoting High-Ticket Products on Facebook

My name is Feza Sengul and I am from London, UK. I've been with the company for less than 6 months and have earned over $40,708. My best month was $15,051.28 and I just smashed my record and earned $9187.30 in one day. My main source of traffic is Facebook status updates and I have not spent a cent on advertising. I'm sure I'll have even better success when I invest in paid traffic.

Before MOBE, life was not easy. My parents grew up on a farm in the mountains of Eastern Turkey. They came to London in the early 1970s. When I was born we lived in a council estate in Northolt. Being the youngest of 5 boys I would often inherit clothes that were too big. I was a very shy boy and lacked self-confidence growing up. After college, I was able to find a job in IT recruitment but wasn't happy. I chased the dream of making more money in network marketing but the profit margins were too small and the volume needed to be successful was impossible.

I discovered Matt Lloyd and liked how he teaches that you can't get rich selling cheap products or services. Before joining MOBE one of my brothers said "it's a scam." I ignored him and took a leap of faith and am now earning a 5-figure monthly income. I have never experienced this level of success in my life. Within my first 3 months, I also qualified for the MOBE Motors program and was rewarded with a new Audi A4 S-Line! (Details about MOBE Motors at: www.mobemotors.com) This is by far the best online business model I've ever seen.

Feza Sengul (Diamond Member)

It always amazes me when I meet people who call themselves Internet marketers, yet don't have a Facebook account. All your prospects are there, along with *1.4 billion others*. Can you imagine that?

The average user spends over 20 minutes daily on Facebook. Americans and Westerners spend more than twice as long... just on Facebook. That's where their attention is, so you want to make sure you're putting your business in front of them while they are there.

Facebook Fan Pages vs. Facebook Groups: Which is Better?

Think of a Facebook fan page as more of a billboard, where people can leave comments and you can interact, and a Facebook group as more of a community, with you as the leader.

Personally I use both, though I much prefer groups—and private groups at that. If people want to join my Facebook group, they must request access, and can't come in until I approve them. It's like my own private club, where I'm the bouncer. And if anyone misbehaves, I can kick them out, too.

Inside your group, you're free to talk about whatever you like, in any way you like, but try to keep it relevant to whatever it is you're promoting. If you're promoting weight-loss products, you wouldn't start talking about dating products, would you? Similarly, if you are promoting dating products, then don't talk about gardening.

In my groups, I talk about business: About getting more leads for your business, scaling, hiring, having the right mindset... those kind of things. I try to share useful, valuable content 70% or more of the time. For example, sometimes I'll be watching videos on YouTube about inspirational entrepreneurs who became billionaires—and I'll take 30 seconds to go to my Facebook group to share the link and urge others to watch. The other 30% of the time, I promote my websites. I may have a live event coming up in a month's time, so I'll promote it. Or I may have a live webinar in a few nights time, which I'll promote—and on that webinar I may be selling a course for a few thousand dollars.

You're the leader in your group, so act accordingly. You can ask for opinions, but be firm. Be the authority figure. You won't see me ever asking for permission, being apologetic, or only expressing safe opinions. Those who try to appeal to everyone appeal to no one. People want leadership—they don't want to follow someone who acts as though they doubt themselves or their own abilities.

Here are some examples of posts I've done over the past few months:

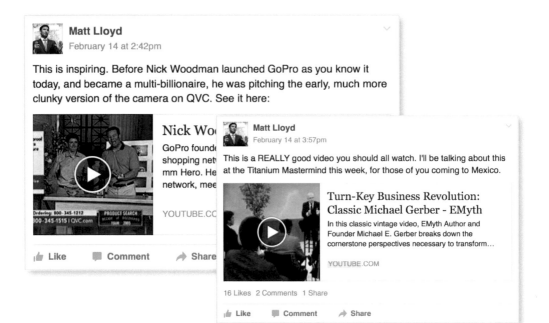

You can join one of my main Facebook groups at **www.facebook.com/groups/mattlloyd**, and observe how I market to the 18,000+ people there.

I also have a Facebook fan page, which you can like / follow at: **www.facebook.com/mobe.official**

How To Get Better Results By Single-Tasking

The average person can learn only one skill at a time. If you start trying to learn too many skills at once, you spread yourself too thin and won't put enough focused effort into one area to get good at it. In order to build an online business, there are a lot of moving parts—a lot of new skills to learn, like getting traffic, writing emails, and much more.

I'm convinced that the biggest cause of failure for new internet marketers is trying to do too many things at once. In fact, that's a chief cause of failure in all small businesses. So stop trying to do it all, and focus on doing one thing at a time. Studies show that, at most, only 3% of the population can effectively multi task. Chances are, you're not one of those three in a hundred. You can, however, break your tasks up into time blocks so that you place ads for an hour, then work on crafting a good email for the next hour, then watch some more training on your chosen traffic method for another hour. But never try to do all 3 activities at the same time, switching from one to the next, to the next. You're not going to be effective! There's a reason I chose to come to this hotel for 3 nights to focus on writing this book; I knew that if I tried to do it along with all my other daily tasks, it would never get done. Approach your business the same way.

The Insider Rules To Making Money Online

One of my idols, Warren Buffet, says, *"If you're at a poker table and haven't figured out who the patsy is after 30 minutes, then you're the patsy."* Usually there is an insider's game being played, which the outsiders are completely oblivious to. Las Vegas and the gambling industry are built upon it. So is the stock market… and to some extent, so is Internet marketing. That's why one of the first things we teach new MOBE affiliates when they start, are the insider rules to doing well in affiliate marketing.

Here are the four basic states people go through when learning any new skill, including affiliate marketing:

- **Unconscious Incompetence**. You don't know what you don't know. This is where most people get in trouble.

- **Conscious Incompetence.** You know there are some things you don't know, and that you need to learn.

- **Conscious Competence.** What you know you're good at. If you're new at something, this amount of knowledge is usually small. And then there's:

- **Unconscious Competence.** You know something so well you can do it without even thinking. You've heard someone say *"I know that place like the back of my hand,"* or *"I could do that with my eyes closed."* That what I mean here.

Let's examine each of these stages in more detail.

When you start out in affiliate marketing, you don't know what you don't know. That's why it's good that you've read this far. You're clearly aware that there's knowledge you don't have, so you're investing in getting the right knowledge so you can become competent. Keep doing that.

Consider traffic, for example. If you're brand-new, you won't even be aware of how little you know. That's Unconscious Incompetence. But as you begin to go through training, like what we teach in the 21 steps when you join the MOBE high ticket affiliate program, you'll become conscious of the fact that there's knowledge you don't know: that is, you enter Conscious Incompetence.

At first, you may feel overwhelmed (this is perfectly understandable, and to be expected). But as you begin to implement what you learn, and make mistakes, readjust, and improve your skills, you become Consciously Competent. You'll still have to concentrate as you place ads and generate clicks... but at least you'll know what you're doing. People ONLY get to this stage if they're willing to take action. Most people never take action at all, so they get stuck at the Consciously Incompetent stage.

With enough practice, you will become Unconsciously Competent. This is like the Olympian athlete who is so good at what they've been practicing for a lifetime, that it seems natural. Unless they can remember what it was like starting out, many of them have trouble teaching others who are brand-new how to do what they do.

When it comes to Internet marketing, I'm now mostly in the Unconscious Competence zone. Not completely. When I go online each day, my actions almost automatically produce large amounts of money. I know exactly what I need to do, and unconsciously know what I *don't* need to do. But it wasn't that long ago that I was just starting out, so I still remember what it's like for someone who is new—which allows me to effectively teach others.

In the very beginning, focus on doing the things that will bring in the cash. Cash has to be your number one priority.

So what are these things which you should be doing, and not doing?

In the very beginning, focus on doing the things that will bring in the cash. Cash has to be your number one priority.

I realize that sounds obvious, but here's the thing: In my experience, most people just don't get it. They get caught up in doing busy work, instead of *productive* work. They want to design a website with a new fancy logo, get business cards made up, register the business, and buy all the things they're going to need to run their new business. And then they want to buy books and courses so they can study and learn everything before taking any action. Before they know it, several months have gone by and they haven't made a cent because they've been spending all their time "getting ready to get ready." This is pretty much what I did for my first year online.

The Danger Of 'Learned Helplessness'

For the new business owner, especially someone who is coming from an employee mentality where they are used to getting paid just for showing up, focusing on activities that don't directly bring in cash can be extremely dangerous. After a certain amount of time goes by without money coming in, they begin to doubt themselves and question their abilities as a business owner. They begin to think that no matter what they do, nothing is going to work.

They begin to develop what's called "learned helplessness."

Back in the 1960s, when the experimental moral boundaries were less strict, a man named Seligman and his colleagues conducted an experiment with dogs and an electric floor. Every time one of the dogs would step outside a circle, it would get a small but painful electric shock. It soon began to associate stepping outside that circle with pain. Its thought process became: *"If I want to avoid getting shocked, it's best I stay within the boundaries of my circle."* Even when the electric charge was turned off, food was offered outside the circle, and there was no risk of getting shocked, the poor dog would just lay there, whimpering, unable to move.

Time and time again, I see people like this, who try to build a business but are afraid to take action—because everything they've tried before hasn't worked. All they have seen is time, effort, and money flow out, with nothing coming in. They begin to question themselves and automatically assume that nothing will work. This is a really dangerous cycle to get yourself into. Throughout most of 2009, I was stuck in this cycle. I'd spent the better part of a year trying to build my new online business. I stayed excited because there were people who were making tens of thousands of dollars a month in the business; other affiliates like me. The record belonged to a South African man who happened to live in my hometown of Perth, Australia. He'd made over $270,000 in a single month!

That amount of money was mind boggling to me back then, so hearing those kind of numbers kept me going. I knew that if I could one day get to that level, then it would all be worth it. But after nine months of full-time effort with literally zero results to show for it, I really began to question myself—especially when those around me were also questioning me. I had plenty of friends and family telling me I was wasting my time, that I should *"quit this online business thing and go back and finish my studies."*

Looking back through the eyes of experience, I know my lack of results had nothing to do with the business. It was all me.

I was focusing on all the wrong things. I was constantly jumping from one shiny object to the next, ignoring the fundamentals of what actually produced a sale. That's why I emphasize the point of going straight for the cash with the HTAM Method in all my MOBE activities, and everything I write. When you are constantly changing directions because you keep thinking you've discovered "the Holy Grail", whether it's a traffic "hack," buying a new course, or testing out some new 'secret software,' you end up taking an overly long path to your goal, which is to get a customer.

It looks like this:

When this is your business strategy, you're lucky if you ever arrive at Point B. Many entrepreneurs don't. They make things much harder than they need to be. It doesn't matter what you're doing; if you go too long without seeing any results, you're going to question yourself, and instead of thoughts of optimism and excitement, your mind will fill with cynicism, resentment, and even anger.

This is the much shorter, easier, faster, and more profitable path you want to take:

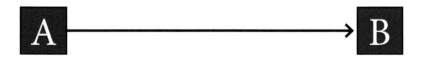

So now we must ask another million-dollar question; right now, in your business, what is the shortest path to making a sale? If you had an hour to make a sale right now, or something really bad was going to happen— what would you do? I suspect you would:

- First identify who is most likely to buy the product you're promoting right now as an affiliate.

- Find out where those people are online (which websites they already visit).

- Go buy some ad space there.

- Start getting traffic.

It sounds so simple…. and it is! But most people prefer to overcomplicate it, and take the much longer path between Point A and Point B.

Financial Freedom and the Mediocre Masses

I remember when I was eight, and I decided I wanted to learn to play the piano. We had this old piano in our lounge room that had been passed down through two generations, so I told my Mum, and she started to teach me. She herself didn't play much, so within six months she found me a proper piano teacher. Her name was Mrs. Cashmore. Once a week, we'd drive an hour out to her farm so I could get my lessons. Mrs. Cashmore was an excellent teacher. She gave all her students a 'timesheet,' where we'd commit to how much we were going to practice each day for the next 30 days. It didn't matter if it was for 30 minutes or for 2 hours; the important thing was that it got done. After each day's practice session, I had to get my timesheet signed by my mum, to prove to Mrs. Cashmore that I'd done the practice.

If we did all our practice sessions each day for the minimum required time, without missing a day, then each week we'd get a reward. The whole routine taught me a valuable lesson; set a daily target, and be disciplined in executing it. Even when you don't feel like doing it, you do it. That's what discipline is all about.

But most importantly, I learned the value of practice. When I first started to play, I was terrible. I hit all the wrong keys. My timing was off. But after several years of disciplined, daily practice, I started to get good. I entered contests where I played against dozens of others on a similar level from all around my state. And I *dominated* those contests. It was rare that I didn't get First or

Second Prize. But my success didn't come from natural talent. It came from disciplined, hard work. I put in more focused hours than just about anyone else to train my body and mind to play well. That's how you get good at anything, and that's how you're going to get good at online affiliate marketing.

There are a lot of affiliate marketers out there, and most of them form what I like to call "the mediocre masses." They get mediocre results, because they put in a mediocre effort. They try something for a day or two, and when they don't see immediate results, they move on to the next shiny object and try that. After a few weeks or months of mediocre results, they give up. They give up way too easily. Don't make that mistake! Never sell yourself short! It's going to take you some time to get good at affiliate marketing, to the point where you can consistently generate commissions daily and create true financial freedom. But if you practice it with the same discipline as you would practice a new musical instrument, you *will* get good!

If you want to know my secret to selling over $100 million dollars' worth of my programs online over the last few years, I'll tell you: I work harder, I'm more focused, and I'm more disciplined than my competitors. I've put in a lot more hours of practice. That's all there is to it. Plus, the competitiveness within me wants to beat the other guys; I enjoy beating them. I'm not in business to make friends, I assure you. Ray Kroc, the man who built McDonalds to great heights, once said, *"If any of my competitors were drowning, I'd stick a hose in their mouth and turn on the water."*

From the very start, this was how I approached Internet marketing. I remember going to an Internet marketing event in San Diego back in 2010, and having to share a room with another guy I'd met on Facebook who was also there (neither of us could afford the hotel room ourselves at that stage). One of the strategies we learned at that event was to write a blog post every single day. So we were in the room talking about this, and he told me that he was going to "try" doing it when he got home. I also wanted to do it, but after thinking about it for a second, I told him that instead of doing just one, I was going to write 10 blog posts a day. I figured that if I wanted to be in the top 1% of affiliate marketers, I had to be willing to outwork 99% of them.

If you want above-average results, you've got to be willing to put in an above-average effort.

Read that again. Remember it.

Is all this talk of putting in above-average effort scaring you? Or at least, slightly deterring you? If it is, I've got some great news for you. The average effort put in by the average affiliate marketer is exactly sweet F$%@ All. Excuse my language, but that's the best way to describe it. I'm continually disappointed at how little effort people will put into learning affiliate marketing before they give up. But then I think about how much easier their lack of effort makes my job, and I cheer up.

For you to get above-average results, you only need to outwork the average person... and that's really easy. Here's what I mean: the average affiliate marketer puts in less than 30 minutes of work a day when they get started. Most never even place their first ad before they quit—and keep in mind that if you don't place an ad, you can't get traffic, and you have no hope of getting paid. An affiliate marketer is by definition someone who drives traffic to other people's offers—so without the traffic part, you can't call yourself an affiliate marketer. Most newbies spend the majority of their time watching training courses and never taking any action. I'm not saying watching training videos is bad, but if you never implement what you learn, then no amount of training will bring you results.

The average person tells themselves things like, "if it's so easy to make money with affiliate marketing, then everyone else would be doing it. Therefore, since not everyone makes money with it, it can't be easy, and there's no point in me even trying." That's what they call a "self-fulfilling prophecy."

If you've read this far, you're already doing better than the average person. So keep reading, and actually implement what I'm teaching you—I dare you!

CHAPTER TEN

The Highest Paid Skills in the World

T he two highest-paid skills in the world are sales and marketing, hands down. As a business owner, sales and marketing must be your main focus *at all times* no matter what level you're at. Even after hitting $100 million in revenue, my main role in running MOBE is to continually improve our marketing. This is what gets us new business, and ensures our affiliates continue getting paid the maximum commissions.

It never stops.

In this chapter, I'll explain the difference between sales and marketing and the fundamentals of both. You'll learn:

- **The Difference Between Sales And Marketing…** and which one is more important to learn.

- **A Simple 3-Step Sales "Formula" That Works Every Time:** Master this simple formula, and you'll be ahead of 99.9% of your competition.

- **How To Outsource Time-Consuming Tasks for $8/Day:** You should outsource everything that draws your attention away from sales and marketing.

- **The Purpose Of Your Business (A Reminder):** Never lose sight of your real goal… financial freedom.

Let's get started…

The Difference Between Sales And Marketing

So, what's the difference between the two highest-paid skills in the world? I define marketing as *salesmanship to the masses*. Getting good at sales on an individual basis will make you a much stronger marketer. I learned that in a telemarketer job in 2008, which I put myself into in order to learn how to sell. Cold-calling customers, getting sworn at, and getting rejected all day long—it really toughened me up. I just sat there all day waiting for people to pick up as the calling machine called them one after another, and when someone answered, I launched into my spiel. I got used to rejection and learned not to take it personally; but I also learned how to talk to people and how to sell one-on-one. I *had* to sell, because if I didn't get results, I didn't get paid.

So when I started marketing to the masses, I already knew how to sell to individuals. Marketing is the process of preselling, providing content that naturally leads to a sale. With the right marketing, the offer is positioned properly and the prospect is price-conditioned; that is, they know what the price will be. By the time they've gone through your marketing and get to the point where you're asking for a commitment—either on the phone, one-on-one, or online—there is little resistance involved. They're predisposed to buy. Good marketing makes your job of selling *infinitely* easier.

That's one of my goals with the MOBE affiliate marketing program.

MOBE has a phone sales team, and we have our own event sales team. Both of those channels involve selling in person, but I aim to make my marketing as good as it can be so that when the prospect has gone through our marketing, and they actually get in front of a sales rep, the sales rep's job is easy. I want it to be easy, so we'll have the highest possible conversion rates, and our affiliates make the maximum amount of money possible. There are a lot of businesses out there that have lousy marketing, and focus only on selling. Because they have bad marketing, most of the people they spend one-on-one time with are tough sales. They haven't been educated about why that company's solution is the right one, why it's better than the competition, why it's worth the price tag, and why they need to get it right now.

When marketing is done right, the one-on-one sales part is easy. It's possible to have prospects calling you, credit card in hand, saying, *"I just read through all your information about the XYZ program, and I'm ready to buy. Are you able to help me with that?"* Compare that with the average business owner's uphill experience, where they have to cold call, chase leads down, and beg them to buy. Which would you rather do?

As a rule of thumb, you never want to talk to a lead who hasn't reviewed your marketing materials first. Otherwise, you're starting that interaction from scratch, and you'll waste too much time having to tell and sell. That's not a high-leverage task. Instead, it's better to market to the masses within your niche, and have the most interested prospects identify themselves through their actions (e.g. have them click a link, fill out a form, call you, etc.), so you can follow up with them individually, close the sale, and collect the money.

If you have a choice between getting good at selling or getting good at marketing, choose to hone your marketing skills. Back in 2009, when I started calling the first leads I was generating online, I wasn't very good at selling. I had some skills that I had picked up during my summer in commission-only sales, but I didn't enjoy the process, nor did I have the patience for it. So when I would call a lead, I would usually lose the sale to someone else who could sell better. Unsurprisingly, more of my focus shifted towards getting good at marketing: that is, the preselling. I began doing things like creating irresistible offers—*"Buy this program and I'll give you a 30-minute strategy session valued at $297, where I'll show you how to do XYZ"*—or improving the persuasiveness of my sales copy.

A Simple 3-Step Sales Formula
That Works Every Time

There is a definite order of importance when it comes to selling something online:

1) Choose the Right Audience. It doesn't matter if you hire the best copywriter in the world and pay them $50,000 to write you a sales letter. If you're trying to sell a weight-loss product to people who don't give a damn if they're fat, you're going to have a hard time making sales. The most important factor in whether or not you get sales comes down to choosing the right audience. Always. That is literally over half the battle. As I explained in Chapter 2, you pick the audience FIRST, then sell them the things they want, not vice versa.

To give you an extreme example: If you try to market a product in English to a group of people who speak only Chinese, it doesn't matter how good the copy is; you're not going to make any sales. You literally don't speak the same language. Similarly, if you market a cosmetics product designed to remove facial wrinkles to young men who don't have any (and wouldn't care much if they did), you're not going to make sales. If you market a Louis Vuitton handbag to ladies who prefers to get bargains at the local flea market, you're not going to make sales there, either.

Audience selection (i.e., who is clicking your ads) is your first and most important priority. If you're in affiliate marketing and generating a lot of clicks but making no commissions, this is the most likely reason why. You've picked the wrong audience.

2) Making The Right Offer is the next thing to focus on, and you should make it as irresistible as possible. Your "offer" is basically what you're giving your prospect the option of buying. It can be broken down into:

* Here's what I've got for you.

* Here's what it will do for you.

* Here's what I want you to do next.

If you're going to start "split testing" different variations of sales copy, the first thing you'll want to test before the words is the actual offer itself. Try offering a double-your-money-back guarantee or three high-value, fast-action bonuses long before you start changing the order of words in your headline.

A great offer does the following:

- It's so outrageous and irresistible it can't be ignored.

- It removes as much of the risk for the buyer as possible.

- It asks for so little in return for what's being offered that buying it is a no-brainer.

- It actually makes the buyer feel almost guilty, because they're getting such a good deal at your expense.

The offer that launched Domino's Pizza and grew one of the most successful companies of all time in that niche was: *"Fresh, hot pizza delivered to your door in 30 minutes or less—or it's free."* They had to stop doing that later, at least in the USA, because their delivery guys were in such a hurry they were driving recklessly. But as an offer, it was unbeatable.

3) The Sales Copy comes last. For most people, this feels counterintuitive. They want to do it first, but last is its proper place. That doesn't mean it's not important; it's vitally important. But so often, I see people who think great sales copy is the be-all and end-all of marketing—that great sales copy can sell any product, when in fact it cannot. A lot of copywriters who have never sold their own programs before like to think that copy is king. When they write sales copy for an affiliate launch, and it grosses over $1 million in sales, they think their copy was solely responsible. It wasn't. More often than not, it was more due to the fact that the affiliates promoting the launch had built up a strong relationship with their lists, to the point that their recommendation was the main driver of all the sales.

When you have a really great product and a great offer, sales copy becomes even less important. Think back to when the first iPods came out. Before then, a good mp3 player could only store about 30 songs. Most were not being marketed that well.

Apple came up with the iPod, and presented it as *"a thousand songs in your pocket."* And because it really worked, and the message was so compelling, Apple revolutionized the mp3 player market.

Those are the top three requirements for effective copy. Now, does all this sound like a lot of work? Good, because it is. Researching what a market really wants, creating the product, finding the copywriter, then building all the web pages needed to create a sales funnel—there's a lot involved. And then you still need to get merchant accounts, handle customer service, fulfillment, and hundreds of other little things. Worse yet, it's possible to do all of that and still miss the mark, producing a dud that doesn't sell—and there goes several months (or years) of your life. That's why most people who want to make money online decide to do affiliate marketing. You let someone else create the products and sales funnels. You let them drive traffic first, and make sure it converts. And only then do you start sending traffic so you can make commissions.

So if I scared you a little by explaining product creation and all of that, don't worry; you don't need to go down that path, and you can still make a great full-time income online. Just become an affiliate for a good company like MOBE, and promote your affiliate links. You never even have to leave Level 1 unless you want to, and you can still make very good money.

How To Outsource Time-Consuming Tasks For $8/Day

Once you have commissions coming in consistently with your affiliate marketing business, one of your first priorities is duplicating yourself. If you want to keep increasing your earnings each month, and scale into the many hundreds of thousands of dollars a year, you'll need to hire other people to help you. If I hadn't built a team of people to help me run MOBE, there's no way I could have reached over $100 million in sales.

You don't need to spend much money to start doing this. One of the first people I ever hired I paid just $2 an hour. The guy was from Pakistan. He worked about four hours a day, because at the time, that's about all I could afford. He knew absolutely nothing about marketing. At the time, I was running ads on Facebook and targeting the major network marketing companies. So I wanted him to take over placing the ads, because it was a time-consuming process. When I asked, "Do you know what network marketing is?" he gave me some explanation about it having to do with electric circuits!

He knew nothing, but he was able to learn very fast and had a great attitude.

These days, he makes over $100,000 a year in my company, and is easily among my top three most valuable people on the team. He also works hours that rival mine, and it's not uncommon for me to find him in the office at 5 AM in the morning, still working away.

(Athar, if you're reading this—I appreciate you).

By the way, you may be thinking that paying someone just $2 an hour sounds like exploitation. Whether it is or not depends on where the person lives, what their experience and skill level is, and whether they choose to do the work. You're not forcing them to work, after all. You're offering them money for work, and it's completely optional. In some parts of the world, the cost of living is less than $5 a day. That $2 an hour is enough to feed their whole family.

Having said all of that, even where people have advertised on sites like Upwork.com that they'll work for $2 an hour, these days I prefer to pay a lot more. And anyone I ever hired at that rate who proved their value to me quickly got a pay rise.

The first roles you'll want to hire for are for anything that takes your attention away from sales and marketing.

For example, administrative work, like doing your bookkeeping and responding to emails, is something you want to get off your plate as fast as you can. The next role I hired for was customer service. When I got my first customer service rep, I was doing over $40,000 per month. The business had grown very suddenly, and I wanted it to keep growing at that pace. But for several hours a day I was getting bogged down responding to customers on issues like missing login details, providing access to our private Customer Owner Facebook groups, and the odd refund. I'd find myself getting frustrated, because I knew that instead of doing this work (which I could outsource for under $15 an hour) I should be on the phone selling to my best leads and making hundreds of dollars an hour. So I ended up hiring the sister of another Internet marketing guru as my first customer service rep at $12 an hour. Frankly, I had a really hard time paying her that money every week, because I was still thinking with a poverty mindset (like I said, I was new to making a lot of money every month). So I would sometimes find myself spending 30 minutes doing customer service work to save on staff costs. It's not easy to change a lifetime of conditioning about how to think about money. But I did change because I knew I wouldn't start doing much bigger numbers until I became comfortable paying out much bigger numbers.

The next role I hired was my first phone sales rep—a huge turning point. By this stage, I was on the phone most of the day. The money was good (I was approaching $100,000 a month, and this was in early 2012), but I was nothing more than a highly paid hourly worker. I wasn't in business for that; I was in business to create systems that would pay me a lot of money regardless of whether or not I showed up to work. Back then, my entire business model was to sell my "Inner Circle" for $97 as my customer acquisition (front end) product. For that, they got access to my weekly webinar, plus a one-hour consult with me. I was a cheap date back then - not so much these days. After about 45 minutes of consulting, I'd often steer the conversation towards my $2,000 program if I felt it would genuinely help them. Soon, about 1 out of 3 people I was talking to were buying that program; and every time I made a sale, the affiliate who introduced that customer to MOBE would get a $1,000 commission. I would tell the affiliate, and surprise them by publicly posting on their Facebook Wall, *"Congratulations, you just made $1,000 promoting MOBE!"* I still do that to this day, but only if the commission exceeds $3,300.

Since most of the sales calls were to customers in America, and I lived in Australia (which has the opposite time zone), I'd usually start calling around 9 PM, and often be up until about 4 AM. Again, the money was good. Six figures a month running the entire operation out of my bedroom in my parents' house (they had no idea!). But it wasn't sustainable. I was working long days, and was on the phone half the night. I needed to hire someone else to do the sales calls so I could get back to focusing on the marketing. So I started recording all my sales calls (with the permission of the customers, of course) so I could use them as a 'training library' for a sales person.

The first guy I hired for the role was an engineer, who had also been one of my first customers. I'd never met him in person, but had talked to him a few times online and knew he was keen to quit his job and work from home. He was an engineer - not a sales guy. But with the recordings of my sales calls to use as training, he actually did well in the role. Sales went down a little compared to when I was doing it, but now I suddenly had *hours* of extra time in my day, which I could use to focus on generating more leads and customers! A couple of months after that, I hired another salesman. This one had a lot more experience; he was already selling high-end programs for another company in our niche, a company much bigger than mine which was run by 4 guys. Ironically, those 4 guys joined MOBE as an affiliate several years later, and have made many millions of dollars in commissions. When I hired him, I prepared myself for sales to drop. I knew he was good, but I thought, *"He's not going to be able to convert like me, selling to my own leads."*

But I was wrong! Not only was he better than me, he was better by a huge margin. It wasn't good for my ego; but it was good for my wallet. I remember the first time he ever sold two of the new high-end programs we'd just launched, for a combined price tag of $24,000. When you're doing a couple hundred thousand dollars a month, you don't need to add too many $24,000 transactions each month to watch your monthly income rise fast. My eyes were really opened at that point. Nowadays, sales of those programs are a daily occurrence—and every time we sell them, some MOBE affiliate is getting paid a total of $8,800 in commissions.

From that point on, I began to hire people for our tech team, finance team, event team, and many other areas as well. I haven't stopped hiring since.

The Purpose of Your Business (A Reminder)

Always keep the purpose of your business in mind. Never forget why you're doing this. Surprisingly, many business owners forget this (or never accept it in the first place). But here's the secret:

At the end of the day, you're in business to create financial freedom.

Many of you reading this are here to get rich, and that's fine. The highest-paid athlete in the world, boxer Floyd Mayweather, has a lot of critics, but one of the things I respect about him is that he was in boxing to make money, and he admits it. His career wasn't about the glory of beating the very best at the height of their careers. His goal was to get to end of his career with full health and minimum damage, while making the maximum amount of money.

After his biggest fight with Manny Pacquiao, he walked away with over $210 million for 36 minutes of work—*$5.8 million a minute*. The fight had been built up over the course of five years, to the point that when it was announced, Pay Per View records were smashed and Las Vegas was overrun with fans who were willing to pay thousands of dollars each to see the fight. With total career earnings of over $700 million upon retirement in September 2015, his record as the third-highest earning athlete of all time is going to be very hard to beat (Tiger Woods has made $1.4 billion, and Formula One race car driver Michael Schumacher $800 million). He may very well make a comeback and earn even more money.

Will Floyd Mayweather go down in history as the greatest boxer who ever lived? No. Will he go down in history as the greatest business strategist of the sport? Absolutely. Without question. He has said, unashamedly, *"I'm in the prize fighting business—I fight for the money."* He knew what business he was in. There's nothing wrong with getting into business to make money. Never think otherwise. I hear business gurus espousing their flowery 'feel good' advice about the purpose of starting a business, and I just roll my eyes. One of them, whom I happen to know well, loves to say publicly how he's only in business to "help people." Yet behind closed doors, he's one of the most money-hungry, ruthless sales guys I know!

Never lose sight of the fact that you're here first and foremost to make a profit.

So, do you focus on making money, or helping people? It doesn't have to be one or the other; it can be both. You can make money through helping people. As Zig Ziglar says; *"You can have everything in life you want, if you will just help other people get what they want."*

Too many people leave out the part about getting what they want.

Never lose sight of the fact that you're here first and foremost to make a profit.

So, I ask again: What business are you really in?

A mentor of mine—someone I pay well over $10,000 a month to speak to for one hour a week (and who also speaks at our Platinum Mastermind events from time to time)—once ran a $250 million per year seminar operation. He was in the real estate training business before the big crash in 2008. Each month, 60,000+ students attended his seminars around the world, and he had over 2,000 employees. I remember flying out to his office in Florida to spend a few days consulting with him. I had recently launched my own training seminars, and while they were doing well, I wanted to take them to the next level. After the normal pleasantries, we sat down across from each other, he looked me right in the eye, and he asked, *"What business are you in, Matt?"*

I thought about it for a moment, knowing he wanted a certain answer, and not wanting to get it wrong. "I'm in the money business," I replied confidently.

"No. What business are you in?"

I replied, this time almost as a question... "I'm in the marketing business?"

"No. What business are you in?"

Finally, I gave up. "I don't know anymore," I said jokingly.

And he replied, "You're in the 'putting butts in seats' business."

He went on to explain that my main role in running a seminar business was to get people to actually attend. If I couldn't do that, then I wouldn't be able to build a successful seminar business. I wouldn't be able to attract the best speakers, I wouldn't be able to attract a good road crew, and most importantly, I wouldn't be able to run profitable events. Events aren't cheap to put on. Depending on the size, they can easily cost $20,000 or more. The most expensive event I ever put on was my Titanium Mastermind event at the Atlantis resort in the Bahamas. Over $500,000 all up - it almost killed me! Without being able to consistently and predictably get butts in seats, the economics of the seminar business doesn't work. So my entire role was to craft marketing campaigns that kept seminar rooms full. My role was not to be on stage at every event, providing the content. Even though I do still train and speak at my really high-end events, there are plenty of other talented trainers I can hire. The one role that's hard to outsource is putting butts in seats. If most people knew how to do it well, they'd be very rich.

So now I'm going to ask you, as a new affiliate marketer: *"What business are you in?"*

You're NOT in the business of posting fancy blogs. You're NOT in the business of designing logos. You're NOT in the business of learning HTML so you can build your own websites. You can hire people to do all that, usually pretty cheaply.

Again... never forget that you're here first and foremost to make a profit.

When you start getting distracted, come back and read this section a few times, and remind yourself what business you're truly in.

CHAPTER ELEVEN

Scaling Your Business

I f you want to keep on making more and more money each month with your affiliate business, you need to get good at scaling. I touched on this concept in Chapter 4, when I discussed feeding the stallions.

One of my biggest beliefs is that I never want to get comfortable in business. Comfort leads to complacency, which has killed more businesses than corporate raiders and the Great Depression combined. Even if you told me you're happily making $50,000 a month, I'd tell you to focus on making more. It's not about the money. It's about achieving your innate potential. If you feel guilty about all the extra money you're making, then feel free to donate it all to charity. And then keep making more.

In this chapter, I'll share some lessons I've learned while scaling MOBE to a $100 million company. You'll learn:

- **How To Achieve Your True Potential...** including how to leverage fear (in a healthy way) to avoid complacency.

- **Scaling And The Dangers Of Making "Too Much" Money:** An important reminder to watch your "net" sales, not just gross sales.

- **A Day In The Life Of A 6-Figure Affiliate Marketer:** What to do and what NOT to do in a typical day to hit $100,000/year.

- **How To Scale Up To Even Bigger Numbers**

Let's get started...

As you scale your business, your email list will become a valuable asset. Monetize it by promoting the offers in my HTAM system and get paid commissions of $1,250 to $10,000 (or more)! Sign up at **www.fivefigureaffiliatemarketing.com**.

How To Achieve Your True Potential

I'm convinced that the majority of the population never come close to achieving what they are truly capable of. That's why I'm so hard on the few people I actively mentor 1-on-1. I want them to see within themselves what I see within them. So I try to push them beyond their limits.

It's also why I've somewhat "checked out" of normal society and prefer not to mix with others. I don't watch TV or read the newspaper anymore. I don't enjoy social get-togethers with strangers—most of the things they talk about, and their aspirations, just seem so trivial. They want to complain about such petty things as the rising costs of fuel, politics, what Sarah said about John during lunch break, and what's on TV tonight.

What a waste of time. What a waste of *life*.

But I do enjoy being around other entrepreneurs. They, like me, see endless possibilities. They're all about finding solutions, not focusing on the problems, and they want to achieve their full potential. That's why I like hosting live training events for other entrepreneurs like the Titanium, Platinum, and Diamond Masterminds.

Titanium Mastermind Bahamas

Here's how you avoid getting comfortable and keep on scaling; besides wanting to better your best, *you leverage fear* - fear of the competition, and fear of losing what you have. Having fear for both is healthy. Not that long ago, there were times when my bank account was completely drained, and I didn't know how I was going to pay the rent. Within me, there is definitely some fear and paranoia about losing it all. But now I welcome it, and think of it as a good thing. It's what keeps me on my toes. If I don't feel occasional periods of stress and exhaustion, then I know I'm not pushing myself hard enough.

Money is how you keep score in business. Not just with your competition, but mainly with yourself. Every month you should try and better your best. That's how I got to where I am now. Many of the affiliate marketers who were at the top of their game when I started are gone—because they lost the hunger they had when starting out. They made some money, got comfortable, became lazy... and then guys like me soared right past them. Don't let this happen to you. When you make your first commission, celebrate—but not for too long. Go get the next commission.

Usually what happens to newly successful affiliate marketers, is they make a few commissions and then settle into a routine. They never scale. Some are comfortable at $70,000 a year, and can't get past it. Others, at $100,000 a year. Some even take it up to $500,000 a year. But sooner or later, most people hit a ceiling, and you probably will too. I hit them from time to time myself. But the only way to smash through a ceiling is to never be satisfied.

Scaling and the Dangers of Making "Too Much" Money

I was 25 when I first grossed $1 million in total sales online. It was a huge deal to me—literally years in the making. Of course, I didn't get to keep it all. At the time I had saved a few hundred thousand dollars of it, and it was just sitting in the bank. For the next 12 months I kept hustling, building the business. It was a wild ride, but I was having a lot of fun.

I remember getting to my 26th birthday, and just before it, I crossed over $1 million in actual cash in a bank account. Back then, I wasn't really investing in real estate or other assets like I do now, so it was all just sitting there. To be honest, I didn't really know what do with it all... Although I did enjoy logging into my online banking each day and just staring at it. Over the next five months or so, my business continued to scale. All my focus was on driving gross sales and making sure I didn't go backwards, ever. Every month *needed* to be a record month. If it wasn't, then I wasn't happy.

Now, it wasn't the money itself that was driving me. It was the desire to constantly better my best—to set new levels of accomplishment, and to be the best I could be. And because all of my focus was on gross sales, I stopped logging into my online banking account and checking my cash - I instead just focused on the gross revenue coming in. If you'd had asked me at the time what my profit margins were, or what I was actually netting, I couldn't have told you.

Well, in May of that year, I found out.

I was netting *virtually nothing.*

Even though hundreds of thousands of dollars were flowing through my merchant accounts each month, it was flowing out just as fast. I was spending way too much money on fulfillment, paying ridiculous commissions and bonuses to our sales teams, and many of the traffic campaigns I was running weren't profitable. I'd stopped tracking as closely as I should have—and I paid the price.

Be careful this doesn't happen to you.

It's great to make a lot of money, but if it's leaving your bank account as fast as it's coming in, it's pointless. Focus on gross sales, but also focus on what you're *netting*. Watch it every single day. These days, my company is much bigger than it was back then, but I still have someone on my finance team manually log in to every single bank account we have every day (even Sundays), visually verify how much cash is there, and then report the numbers to me. I'm aware they could do it much easier with accounting software that's reconciled with the bank accounts, but I like the peace of mind I get from knowing someones actually checking inside each bank account to make sure the money is there. Very often, I'll do spot checks myself just to verify the numbers they give me. As one of my mentors says, *"if you want to keep honest people honest, have a check and a balance."*

A Day in the Life of a 6-Figure Affiliate Marketer

When I was starting out in affiliate marketing, I used to wonder what all these gurus and super-affiliates did on a typical day to generate their results. What was their actual routine every time they sat in front of their computer, to bring in hundreds of thousands of dollars a month? You may have wondered the same thing. You may have wondered what I do to bring in hundreds of thousands of dollars a day - and if you come to one of our advanced live trainings like the Titanium Mastermind, I'll tell you. For now, though, you need to learn to walk before you can run. So focus first on doing your first six-figure year.

The first step is to break down your goal down into smaller, achievable milestones.

$100,000 a year = $8,300 a month

Does that number sound achievable to you? Does it scare you? If it does, your current financial thermostat is set too low. Your first few big affiliate commissions will change that.

Then continue to break your goal down into smaller more achievable goals.

$8,300 a month = about $273 a day

In the scheme of things, $273/day is peanuts. And with an online affiliate program like MOBE, it's easily achievable.

Now let's say you're willing to put four hours a day into your business—which you should be doing (at minimum) if you're trying to replace a normal, full-time income. That means you've got 4 hours a day to place ads that bring in the required $273 / day in commissions. That means that every hour you spend must be worth *at least* $68 ($273 / 4 hours = $68). You can't be doing $5 an hour activities and expect to reach your six-figure target.

On the other hand, if you only have two hours a day, then each hour has to be worth at least $137. Or... if you can only work one hour a day, then you need to focus on activities worth $273 an hour and above. So the less time you have, the more selective you have to be about how you use it.

Here are some activities that can be worth $273 an hour (or possibly a lot more):

* **Researching websites** to place ads on that have your type of desired traffic, and recording them on a spreadsheet.

* **Speaking with a good lead about the product you're promoting** and answering their questions before they buy, whether that's in a one-on-one email exchange, through Facebook messages, or even on the phone.

* **Checking your stats**—how many clicks you've gotten in the last 24 hours, and how many sales—then adjusting your ads based on those numbers to optimize your response.

* **Learning more about the traffic method you've decided to master**, and actually implementing along the way, so you get real life experience doing it.

* **Attending a live event with other affiliate marketers**, and making connections with people at a more advanced level than you... people that you can learn from and joint venture with down the line.

* **Creating duplicatable systems/processes** for lower-value activities and offloading them to other people, so you can focus on higher leverage activities.

Meanwhile, here are some activities that are certainly NOT worth $273 an hour:

- Seeing what your friends and family are doing on Facebook.

- Checking email.

- Watching videos on YouTube that have nothing to do with building your business.

- Organizing stationary and setting up a new printer.

- Watching yet another sales video from an Internet marketing guru about the latest "traffic loophole" they just discovered.

- Checking your email again ("Hey, maybe something important just came in!")

- Trying to learn Photoshop, so you can design a fancy logo for your business, so you can get business cards printed up and feel important.

- Taking any call that interrupts your current task and lets other people control your agenda.

The problem with time is that it seems to move very slowly in the moment. But as you know in hindsight, it moves incredibly fast. Each hour you waste is an hour you'll never get back. So guard your time, and constantly ask yourself the question: **"Is what I'm doing now worth $X?"**, where X = *your desired hourly income to reach your targets*. If the answer is no, then stop doing it, and do something that is. In fact, I recommend you write that question out on a sticky note and put it on the side of your computer screen. **Do it right now**—it will help you.

Now, just because an hour of your time now needs to be worth $X/hour, it doesn't mean that you suddenly stop doing activities worth less than that. There is a process of transitioning into higher-dollar activities. It takes time. How much depends on how quickly you learn, and how fast you're willing to let go of low-level activities to focus on the higher leveraged ones.

How To Scale Up To Even Bigger Numbers

If you plan to make a fortune in MOBE, you must scale up rapidly—and that means placing an ever-increasing value on your time. I do the same calculations as you to help me reach my financial targets, just on a much bigger scale.

Let's say I want to produce $150 million in revenue in the next 12 months, which isn't that far off my actual target for this year. That means that every month, the business must average $12,500,000 in revenue, which works out to about $409,836 a day, or about $29,274 an hour (based on a 14-hour workday).

Now, do I always work 14 hours a day? No. Some days I work less, some days I work more. To me, it's not really work. I love what I do so much that I can't imagine what else I'd be doing with my days if MOBE were not here. It has become my life—though people keep telling me that once I get a wife, that's all going to change. So I'm staying single for now!

I consider an hour of my time very precious. That's why I utterly refuse to do things that can be done for a much lower hourly rate. Like shopping. Or getting Starbucks. Or taking clothes to the dry cleaners. Or letting other people interrupt my day with petty requests. It's also why I had a hole cut through the floor of my apartment and into the office below, and had a custom spiral staircase built. My time is too valuable to me to have to waste it every time I want to get from one room to the next! I put a gym in the corner of my office, instead of taking the elevators two minutes down to Level 3 to use the building's gym, for the same reason.

I've figured out how to generate large sums of money; but for all my wits, I still can't figure out the puzzle of creating more time. So for now, I'll continue to be very protective of it to ensure I'm focused only on high leverage activities. You should do the same.

CHAPTER TWELVE

How the HTAM Method Can Change Your Life

R unning MOBE keeps me pretty busy. But every so often, I sit back in my chair, and reflect upon all the lives that have been changed with our affiliate program.

For example, there's Diamond member Carolina Millan, from Chile. The first time I spoke to Carolina was when I sold her the MOBE License Rights Program in 2012. She was afraid to invest the money, because she doubted her own ability to do well. But at the last minute she decided to go ahead —and three years later, her life has been completely transformed. Then there's Shaqir Hussyin (Diamond member), already a successful Internet marketer, who has earned more than $2,700,000 using this system. And dozens of others who have joined the $100,000 club in the last few years.

I could tell you stories like these for hours. In fact, I have included a number of MOBE success stories as Appendix IV to this book, with links to about 100 more. The impact this affiliate program has had on the Internet marketing industry has been enormous; it's hard to overstate it. And now it's your turn.

In this chapter, I'm going to invite you join the MOBE high ticket affiliate program (again) and answer some nagging questions that may be holding you back. If you've already joined, then I look forward to meeting you in person at one of our live events! If not, read on. You'll learn:

Get access to the ultimate HTAM (High Ticket Affiliate Marketing) system, which pays you up to $13,500 per sale at **www.fivefigureaffiliatemarketing.com**. You will also be assigned a personal HTAM coach, who will walk you through a simple, 21 step training program that shows you how to get started.

- **Why I Want You To Become A MOBE Affiliate**

- **How To Silence The Self-Defeating Voice In Your Head**

- **Answers to the Most Common Questions About MOBE**

Let's get started…

Why I Want You To Become A MOBE Affiliate

There's a reason I've spent the entire weekend locked up in my hotel room writing these words to you. It's because I'm looking for new affiliate partners.

As you know, MOBE has done over $100 million in revenue.

Right now I'm 28 years old, and I have five years invested into MOBE, and seven years invested into Internet marketing… and I'm not quitting, ever. There's no "exit strategy" where one day I'll take the company public, or sell it off to another company. This is a labor of love for me. Every waking hour, I am consumed with making MOBE the best company it can possibly be, with the best high-ticket affiliate program in the world. I'll continue to relentlessly pursue that goal for the foreseeable future—probably until I die. People have told me that I should "slow down" and "not burn myself out." But when you love what you're doing as much as I love MOBE, it's not considered work. Everything else more closely resembles work to me. Running MOBE is where I'm most happy. I want to take MOBE to $1 billion in sales in the shortest amount of time possible, and then I want to take it to $10 billion in sales. And more.

There's no final destination for how far I want to take MOBE. I want to take it as far as I can. But I can't accomplish this on my own. I need your help reaching this goal. I want MOBE to become the Number #1 training resource for small business owners in the world. This is what I call "The MOBE Mission." It's an ambitious goal; some may say impossibly ambitious. But that's what MOBE will become.

To do that, we need several things to happen:

- **We must have better training programs for business owners and entrepreneurs** than any other company. Our training must be clearer, more relevant, more effective, and better than what others offer.

- **We must treat our clients better.**

- **We must reward our affiliates better.**

- **We must get new affiliate partners.**

So I'm extending an invitation to you to join the MOBE high ticket affiliate program at: **www.fivefigureaffiliatemarketing.com**

Remember, we're the only program in the world that leverages the HTAM Method and sells high-ticket sales on the backend FOR YOU and pays you large commissions on them.

This is the moment of truth. This is where you'll either make a decision that can set you free, or continue along another path, oblivious to what could have been.

How To Silence The Self-Defeating Voice In Your Head

Where you are today, right now—your financial situation, your relationships, where you live, everything—is all a result of decisions you've made up until this point.

In late 2008, I made one of the most powerful decisions of my life. I decided to invest a few thousand dollars in an online business program. This was after being pitched for an hour on a live webinar, and then called on the phone by the person who generated me as their lead. I remember having a lot of doubt, and a lot of questions about the program. It sounded like something I could do. It sounded *easy.*

But there was that little voice in my head that had been put there by many years of conditioning from my parents, the media, and society in general. You know the one: *What if this doesn't work? What if you invest the money, then discover it's harder than you thought? Most businesses fail. What makes you think you'll be any different? I'm sure the people getting results have a lot more money/experience/talent than I do, so I probably won't be able to do this.*

But then I thought about it in a different way. I asked myself, *"At the end of my life, will I look back on this decision to try to build an online business, and live an extraordinary life as a result of that business, with no regrets even if I fail? Or, will I be glad that I at least tried?"*

The answer was obvious, so I made the decision to buy right there in that moment. With some lingering fear and excitement, I pulled out my credit card and purchased. In my first few weeks with that program, it was all new to me. I'll be honest with you: the learning curve was steep. But I took it one step at a time, and slowly but surely I began to see results.

I often ask myself how my life may have been different had I listened to that little self-defeating voice in my head. I know that I'd have a LOT less money. I'd probably be working in a finance job I hated. Each day, I'd go to work and come home, and slowly but surely I would accept that was all there was for me.

Did you ever see the movie *Sliding Doors*? In it, the main character is shown living two separate lives as a result of one moment where she took a different course of action. Literally, being a few seconds late to get on a train was the difference between her living out two completely different lives.

Every decision you make can alter the trajectory of your entire life, some a lot more than others. This is one of the biggest decisions you'll ever make. If you decide to move forward and partner with MOBE by joining our affiliate program, then one year from now you could look back on this moment as one of the greatest decisions you ever made.

Also - for those readers in their older years: ***It's never too late.***

Colonel Harlan Sanders started Kentucky Fried Chicken at age 65 after a long career as a gas station owner. Ray Croc was a 52-year-old salesman on the brink of failure when he bought into McDonalds and started building it into the success it is today. GEICO Insurance was started by 50-year Leo Goodwin in 1936, because he wanted people to be able to buy insurance without dealing with brokers. John Pemberton started the Coca-Cola Company at age 55. Jack Weil, CEO of Rockmount, the hugely successful stylish western clothing retailer, started his company in his mid-40s—and ran it until his death at age 107 in 2008.

But before you move forward, you probably have some questions. So let me answer all the most commonly asked ones below:

"Matt you can do this—you're young and good at computers... what about me? I am not from the computer generation and only know the very basics."

This is a question I get from time to time, especially when I'm training at one of our live events like the Titanium Mastermind and some of our more senior students are watching me demonstrate something live on stage. They see how quick I move my mouse, click this button and that, and then in minutes I've set up a new traffic campaign ready to start bringing in leads daily. When they attempt the same, they fumble around at less than 1/10 of the speed, and get frustrated with themselves.

It's very easy for them to think I'm some kind of computer genius. They say, *"Matt, you grew up in the computer generation... I didn't!"* That's true, but first of all, I'm NOT naturally a technical person. When I started, I really struggled to use computers. It's true. In college, I took the most basic computer science class you could take. I ended up getting a score of 51% and barely passing— and to this day, I'm convinced that was only because I made friends with the lecturer and got on her good side. I doubt I actually passed those exams.

These days I'm very proficient at clicking around and doing what I need to place ads, and setting up marketing campaigns. But that's only because I practice every single day. If you're new to this, you may not be able to see yourself placing ads online, watching the cost per click (CPCs) and your click-through rates (CTRs), and adjusting your ad copy to your best advantage (yet). But trust me, with enough practice you'll get good. The main thing is that you learn through *doing*, not by observing and studying courses without ever taking action.

You have to take action. The only way you'll truly learn these new skills is with practice!

I cannot say that enough times, or with enough emphasis. My general rule of thumb is to spend four hours of taking action for every one hour of study.

"Is the market saturated? If there are already quite a lot of MOBE affiliates out there, how am I going to make money?"

I asked the exact same question myself about the company I got started with in late 2008, when I had much more of a 'scarcity mindset.' I remember wanting to know how many other affiliates there were in Australia, where I was living at the time, because I thought that all the easy sales might already have been made. When they told me, "there's about 500 affiliates," I immediately had doubts. "What if those 500 people are all the easiest 500 sales that could be made in the country? What if future sales are going to be much harder?" My thought process back then is now laughable to me today. There are *over 20 million* people in Australia, so 500 is a tiny percentage of the total. And there are *several billion* around the world.

Right now, MOBE is at a similar stage. Sure, we've done over $100 million in revenue. That might sound like a large number, but in the world of big business, it's nothing. It's what some companies spend on their stationary every year (well, maybe not that much, but you get my drift). Given that in the next five years, the amount of people using the Internet is expected to double, and given that MOBE is still doubling and even tripling in our year-to-year growth, I can tell you with confidence we're just starting out. Our major growth phase lays ahead. The amount of customers we've acquired are just a drop in the ocean of potential customers we can still get. I know of one online education marketing

You have to take action. The only way you'll truly learn these new skills is with practice!

company like MOBE that has sold well over *$2 billion* worth of products. MOBE is much smaller, although growing much faster, which is one of the reasons so many people are excited about it.

Like the people who didn't invest in Google stock in early 2008 because they thought it was "overvalued," there will be people who decide not to get involved with MOBE's affiliate marketing program because they think all the easy sales have been taken, and that they missed their window of opportunity. But that window of opportunity just opened up, and it's opened WIDE. It won't be open forever, though; and yes, every day it gets a little smaller. So now's the time to get started.

"Is this one of those pyramid selling schemes?"

No, this is affiliate marketing—the same model used by Fortune 500 companies like Amazon.com to acquire new customers and only pay for results. Online affiliate marketing may be pretty new (only a couple decades old at most), but the concept of a business owner paying someone else a commission to bring them a paying customer is probably about the second oldest profession I'm aware of. It's all around us. When you buy a car or a house, the person who makes that sale usually gets a commission. They're in the business of connecting prospects with sellers, and affiliate marketing operates on the same principles. You're just the middleman.

It's not a business model that's going away any time soon. In fact, as new marketing channels are created (as they are every day), the amount of potential money that can be made in the affiliate marketing industry is going up. Affiliate marketers now have even more places they can place ads, and more places where they can capture the attention of online browsers and get them to click. Just in the last three months, a major new website has become mainstream, and made its creator very rich. This website lets you record videos on your phone and stream them live, where others can vote on the quality of your content. It's already picked up over 10 million new users. It hit its first million users in 10 days. Affiliate marketers are busy figuring out how to promote their affiliate links on it and make a small fortune.

It wasn't that many years ago that affiliate marketers were figuring out how to promote on websites like YouTube, Twitter, and Facebook. Since then, they've collectively made many billions of dollars from each. It's time to get your share of that money.

One more thing… there will *always* be a need for affiliate marketers. The millions of business owners who have products to sell online usually want to focus on their core business, instead of learning how to advertise online. So they're perfectly willing to pay you a percentage of any sales you bring them. Business owners like me are more than willing to be generous with that percentage.

"I read a bad review about MOBE or one of your affiliates - how do I know this is all legitimate?"

Someone close to me recently asked me if I had ever Googled my name or MOBE. I responded, *"Of course. Why do you ask?"* I was then hit with a statement no one ever wants to hear: *"According to a few sites that come up in the search results, you are a scammer."* Now, this person knows me well enough to know that is not true. You can't build a company to the size of MOBE, with many tens of thousands of thousands of clients, by scamming people – and still be in business after all these years. But according to some of the 'reviews' that come up in the search results, MOBE is not a good company.

What you probably don't know, is that behind the majority of these seemingly unbiased 'reviews' are actually on of our main competitors. They write the fake 'scam reviews' about MOBE to funnel the search engine traffic from people doing searches on MOBE, to their company instead. After trashing our company they then recommend their own company, product, or service as the solution. This is not a new trick – people have been doing this ever since the first search engines came out.

I've been aware of these fake review sites for a long time. But rather than focus on them and their false information, I chose to take the high road and ignore them. I put all my focus into making MOBE the best company it can be. Many of these 'scam reviews' follow the exact same structure, and say similar things. That's not a coincidence; the majority of the reviews are from affiliates for a single company, whose founder is among the worst offending parties in terms of the defamatory statements. If you review the training he provides to his affiliates, you'll see he actually encourages his affiliates to go and do reviews on other competing companies (not just MOBE), and then encourages his affiliates to comment on each other's 'review' sites to boost their search engine rankings.

There's nothing wrong with doing reviews on competitors. But when the reviews have false information and make defamatory comments, then it becomes an issue. Most people are intelligent enough to know that it's a competitor desperately attacking my company to get more traffic for their own. Unfortunately there's a huge segment of the market who doesn't have enough online experience to know the difference between legitimate reviews, and these fake reviews. They blindly assume that what they're reading is the truth.

Litigation has always been a last resort for me. Up until this point, I've tried every other way to resolve the issue with this particular competitor. I reached out to them on Facebook, and politely asked to have a conversation about their defamatory blog post. They promptly blocked me – with no response. I also tried calling their phone number many times, to explain politely that they were engaging in defamation, and to respectfully request they take down all their fake reviews. They never answered. They also never responded to the numerous voice messages my team left. After putting up with this one particular company's illegal tactics for long enough, I decided to sue them. At the time of writing, the lawsuit is still ongoing. I anticipate it will cost a lot more money before I finally win, and that's fine with me – over the past few years of growth I've always made sure I kept adequate cash reserves on hand for these kinds of situations, which I knew would eventually arise.

I tell you all this because there's a good chance that whatever negative press you may find on MOBE is usually put out there by competitors. Unfortunately this is a part of the business we are in, where these people sit at home and hide behind their computer screens, and think they can say whatever they want. If you've read this far, then I trust that you can make up your own mind about what kind of a company MOBE is and what kind of a leader I am.

"What am I actually selling with MOBE?"

You're selling educational programs designed to help business owners and entrepreneurs get better results. If you go to Mobe.com and look under the Products link in the menu, you'll see some of the products you'll soon be able to promote and earn commissions on. There are hundreds there already. Someday, there will be tens of thousands. One of my main areas of focus is on creating and acquiring more and more excellent training programs that will help our clients take their businesses to the next level. Whether our clients need help with sales, outsourcing, generating traffic, being more productive, or any of the many aspects of running a business, there will be a training program offered by MOBE that can help them. If you facilitate that transaction by introducing them to us, then you'll get paid a commission. Depending on what you sell, that commission could be a few hundred to many thousands of dollars. Right now, the biggest commission we pay on our most advanced programs is $18,000—which gives you an idea of how well we like to compensate our affiliates.

Besides our training products, we also offer live training events like the Diamond Mastermind, where clients spend several days with us (the longest event currently offered is 10 days), and we work with them on their businesses. We have our big international Mastermind events (Titanium, Platinum, and Diamond), our most valuable and in-depth events, and we also have many three-day live summit events that train on basic to intermediate levels. The Mastermind events are held all around the world—usually in 4 and 5-star resorts in holiday destinations. We've hosted them in places like Fiji, the Bahamas, Costa Rica, Thailand, Curaçao, the Dominican Republic, Indonesia, Malaysia, and Mexico, just to name a few.

As for the three-day summit live events, we do those in main markets like the USA, Canada, the UK, Australia, and all over Asia. We like to host them in places people would want to take their families for a holiday (which many do), so that after the training is done, they can relax and recharge their batteries. These events keep us pretty busy. This coming year, we'll be hosting nine major international Mastermind conferences, close to 60 smaller three-day training events, and many hundreds of smaller two-hour introductory workshops.

....

"If you put yourself out there online, and someone says something nasty about you or what you're doing, how do you handle that?"

....

I figured I'd throw this in, because you're inevitably going to have a few critics along the way, especially once you become successful. You need to know how to deal with them.

There are entire companies out there who have made it their main marketing strategy to bash competing companies (including MOBE), and then recommend their products as an alternative solution. Not only that, once you start building your own email list, you'll have the experience of sending out a broadcast email to all your subscribers, and having one of them respond and call you all kinds of names. These days, I laugh them all off. There is nothing someone can say to me that will offend me or hurt my feelings. The main reason is, they don't know me. The majority of those people are pissed off at the world and will lash out at anyone. So don't make appeasing your critics a focus in your business. Focus on marketing to, selling to, and providing value to your fans.

And you will have fans. Take any group of subscribers, and there will be a segment who really resonate with you. It may be a small segment, but even if just one of out every 100 leads you get likes, trusts, and wants to buy from you, that's enough to build an entire business on.

As for putting your personal details out there, you may be wondering, *"Is it safe?"* Pretty much, in my experience. Only once did I ever have someone show up at my house. He was a happy customer and just wanted to come meet me. These days, I don't put my home address at the bottom of my emails like I used to (instead I put my office address).

Once you get enough exposure online, you may even have the experience of having a complete stranger recognize you while you're out and about. Once, while checking out a resort in the Bahamas for an upcoming event, I had a lady walk up to me and ask, "Are you Matt Lloyd?" Immediately I thought, *Where do I know this woman from, and what's her name?* Turns out she was on my email list and had been happily following me online for years. She asked for a picture and my autograph, like I was some kind of a celebrity, then went on her way.

Grow your business large enough, and this will happen to you.

CHAPTER THIRTEEN

The Start Of A New Beginning

My goal with this book was to explain to you what's important in affiliate marketing, and what's not. And it was to help you avoid making many of the mistakes I made when starting out.

I know you'll make some of them anyway. Just remember that the only thing stopping you from radically transforming your financial life with what you now know, is you. You will determine what happens next.

In this chapter I want to share a special story with you about a period in my life when my family and friends told me I should quit because my new online business hadn't made any money yet (I hope it inspires you).

If It's So Easy, Then Why Isn't Everyone Doing It?

I remember back in 2009, sitting in the passenger seat of my sister's car as she drove to the supermarket, and telling her about the new online business I had gotten involved in—and how my life was going to change. I was so excited. She was skeptical. She had (and still has) a government job, where her contract gets renewed every two years, and she makes an average income. In a slightly patronizing tone, she said to me, *"Matthew, if it's so easy, then why haven't you done it yet?"* And then she asked, *"How much money have you yourself actually made?"*

Her questions bothered me. Not just because she wasn't willing to believe there was a better life than working in a job for the rest of her life, but because

HTAM CASE STUDY

Super Affiliate Ewen Chia Makes over $322,979.55 in the First 15 Months Using the HTAM Method.

My name is Ewen Chia from Singapore and I knew about MOBE for almost 2 years before I decided to join the business.

Initially I was skeptical and decided to do proper research for a long time before taking the plunge in October 2014, first as a Platinum member, then upgrading to Diamond a few months later.

Since joining I've made $322,979.55 in the first 15 months. This translates to a massive 5-figure income every month, part time. My best day and month was on the 12th of August 2015 when I made more than $18,000 in commissions in one day.

I promote MOBE in 2 main ways: 1. Using the time-tested model of email marketing. All I do is set up a squeeze page, and use the materials provided by MOBE to educate and convert leads into a paying customer. 2. Create my own product sales funnel and build MOBE into the backend as a recommendation. For both methods, my main traffic method is simply to buy targeted traffic to my sites, namely with solo ads and pay per click advertising.

Many people are afraid to spend money on traffic, but if you have a positive return on investment (ROI), especially with MOBE, then it makes sense to buy traffic. This gives you faster results.

I decided to join MOBE initially as a way to monetize my websites and to provide an additional source of income, but have since grown to appreciate the training, networking and massive value it provides.

My most valuable advice is to grab the right opportunity when it comes and take action on what you learn!

Ewen Chia (Diamond Member)

I hated to admit that I had not made a single dollar at that point—and we both knew it. I'd spent over $40,000 and many months trying to. But so far, not a single penny had come back. So for the rest of that short ride I sat in silence, frustrated.

Don't ask for advice on starting an online business from people who have never done it.

These were the kind of conversations I'd continue to have over and over in those first few years... not just with family members and friends, but even with my accountant, whom I barely knew! When I told him I was about to invest my life savings into this new online business, and quit university to do it full time, I could see his immediate concern. He strongly advised me not to invest in that business back in 2009, cautioning me that *"these things never work out."* He's no longer my accountant, which is a real shame; I'd love him to see what became of my business!

Here's the lesson for you... don't ask for advice on starting an online business from people who have never done it. In fact, don't ask for advice from people in general, if they have no experience and track record of success in what you're asking about. Otherwise, you're going to get advice that's worth the price you paid: **nothing.**

I refuse to take advice about money from people who don't have any (which is most of the population). When I get advice, I pay a lot of money for it, because I only want the best. The last guy I paid for advice lives in a castle in Scotland. I wired him $60,000 USD for eight hours of his time on the phone. I pay for his advice because he's operated at much higher levels in business than I have (growing a company to a valuation of $450 million at one point in his career). Another guy I pay $10,000 per month to talk to for one hour on Skype once a week, and to also spend two days every quarter with him at his office. This guy built a seminar training company to $250 million a year back in the early 2000's.

For me, advice from people like this is worth paying for. Anyone else, not so much.

Any time I told people about my business back in the early days, they usually offered some encouragement: *"Matthew, it's great that you're doing this business, good for you..."* but then they'd add on something like, *"...but make sure you finish your degree as well—so you've got something to fall back on. It's good to have a back-up plan."*

The moment I heard them say that, I stopped listening.

I'm not faulting them, of course—most were well-meaning, much older people talking to a shy 22-year-old kid who had dreams of making millions. But they didn't get it. If you're going to go into business, you can't have an attitude of, "I'll see how it goes, and if it doesn't work out, then that's okay because I'll have a safety net." You must go in with the mentality of, "I'm going to make this work, *no matter what.*" Because if you don't, you will be derailed at the first few inevitable challenges.

Any time I hear a new MOBE affiliate say something like, *"I'll give this a try,"* I'm tempted to tell them *"Don't bother."* Like Yoda says, *"Do or do not. There is no try."*

And another thing. When it comes to the business of affiliate marketing, there is only one way you can fail, and that's if you quit. Even if you've made no money so far, as long as you're still going, you haven't yet failed in my book. Back in 2009, a group of about 10 of us affiliates began to have weekly meet-ups. We'd meet at the first national seminar for that company in Sydney, and all of us were brand-new. Every week, we'd meet at the Balmoral Pub, a local bar, where we'd get lunch and have a few drinks. We were all so excited about the potential of the business, and how much money we were going to make.

Slowly but surely, fewer people began to show each week. Soon, it was down to just three or four of us. And finally, it was just two of us: me and a woman. Everyone else had given up, or "put the business on hold until later." We were the last two left, and were both still determined to make it work. Well, after one of these meetings, we'd both had a bit too much to drink and got into some kind of argument. I can't even remember what for. She soon quit the business too, and I assumed I'd never see her again. Well, six years, later I got a bit of a shock. Not only did I see her, but it was in the most unlikely of places—on a beach at night in Phuket, Thailand! It was at the welcome dinner for one of my big international training conferences, and she was attending as the guest of one of my MOBE affiliates. I asked her what she was doing these days, and she told me she had gone back to her regular job.

I'm not judging her for that. But we started out together in the exact same place. The only difference was that she chose to give up, and I persisted.

I don't know what you're going to do with the information you get in this book. But don't be the person who gives up. Be the person who persists, and commits to changing their life.

Believe me, it's worth it.

A Final Call To Action

So here's my final advice to you.

Start taking action right now, and commit.

Don't let the inevitable challenges get you down; reframe them as opportunities. Any time you get stuck, and you will, please book a session on your traffic coach's calendar. Ideally, you want to schedule a 30-minute session with your traffic coach twice a week. And don't wait for them to reach out to you—you must reach out to them. When you need help, take full responsibility for getting it, wherever you need it in your business or personal life. Keep in regular touch with your coaches, and at the end of each session, ask, "What are the three biggest things I need to focus on to get my business to the next level?" They'll tell you, and then it's going to be your responsibility to actually go implement them.

Know this, however: your coach is not there to be a cheerleader. Their purpose is to teach you what to do to generate traffic, so you can start earning some commissions. Listen to their advice. Think of them as a driving instructor. They'll be in the passenger seat, coaching you through everything: showing you how to write ads, giving you feedback on your advertising reports, making suggestions about how you can optimize them. But you're steering the vehicle, and you will decide how fast you want to go.

How long you continue to get coaching will be up to you. To this day, I still get weekly coaching myself—though I pay a lot more for it than you'll be paying for a MOBE coach. I have gone through several coaches as my own skills and results have improved, but I still find it very useful to talk to someone with more business experience than me - to review my goals, to make adjustments, and to be held accountable.

Take action right now, and get started as an affiliate with MOBE. You have nothing to lose, and your financial freedom to gain.

Join the MOBE high ticket affiliate program now at:

www.fivefigureaffiliatemarketing.com

Matt Lloyd
Kuala Lumpur, Malaysia
February 2016

The MOBE High Ticket Affiliate Program is the world's best HTAM system that pays you up to $13,500 per sale!

Backend high-ticket sales are made FOR YOU: MOBE does the work and deposits commissions directly into your bank account twice a month!

PLUS ... you get a **personal coach** that will walk you through a simple 21-step training program on how to make your first BIG commission (even if you have zero computer skills!)

90% of the work required to run a business is Done For You:

✓ No products to create

✓ No fulfillment or customer service

✓ No payment processing

✓ No website design or hosting

✓ No sales presentations or funnels to create

✓ No selling in person or over the phone

... It's all Done For You!

Join today at: **www.fivefigureaffiliatemarketing.com**

APPENDIX I
The MOBE Compensation Plan

MOBE offers one of the most generous compensation plans on the market with a large selection of business training products, services, live training events and exclusive masterminds that you can promote for a commission.

To view the full and most recent copy of the MOBE Compensation Plan, please visit: **www.MOBE.com/compensation**

The MOBE Income Disclaimer

The MOBE Compensation Plan is an exciting opportunity that rewards you for selling Small Business Training Resources to customers. You can also benefit by sponsoring other participants who can do the same. Although the opportunity is unlimited, individual results will vary depending on the commitment levels and sales and marketing skills of each participant.

To view the full and most recent copy of the Income Disclosure, please visit:
www.MOBE.com/income-disclosure

Where to Get Help and Support If You're a MOBE Affiliate

Your coach is there specifically to help you with your problems, especially when it comes to learning traffic, choosing offers, and making more money. Be sure to listen to what they say; every coach out there has stories of people who either ignored their advice, or made every excuse in the world not to follow that advice.

You can make money, or you can make excuses. You can't do both.

If you're facing a problem your coach can't handle, like software issues, getting paid promptly, or customer service, then go to **www.MOBE.com/support**. There you'll find answers to hundreds of Frequently Asked Questions, our customer support phone number, and also how to submit a support ticket.

You can also go to **www.mobeaffiliatesupport.com**, where you'll find more recourses that you will need as an affiliate.

MOBE Inspiration: Stories to Inspire You

I n this appendix, I've included only a few of the literally thousands of success stories that people just like you and I have enjoyed when putting the HTAM method into play, armed with dedication and hard work. You can find plenty more at **www.MOBE.com/success**—where you can see our affiliates telling their own tales of their success with MOBE in video format.

. . . .

DARREN SALKELD
DIAMOND MEMBER - WINNIPEG, CANADA

My name is Darren Salkeld from Winnipeg, Canada.

I started with MOBE a little over 2 years ago, 25 months ago to be precise. Knowing the power of being fully positioned, I never hesitated to become a Diamond partner right from day one.

To date, I've been paid over $8,337,218.63 in commissions from MOBE, making my affiliate partner spot the #1 all-time producer globally for MOBE. My best "single week" of paid commissions in MOBE has been $140,352.

Generating 6-figures a week consistently is more money than most will earn in 2-3 years at a regular day job. Believe me, there was a time when I too thought it was all just a fantasy.

You see, before I found online marketing, I used to be a blue collar factory laborer. I grew up on a farm, lived in a mobile home trailer and drove a beat up old pickup truck.

The one thing I had was a strong mindset that drove me to never give up. I knew there was a way to succeed. Discovering the power of Systems, Leverage and surrounding myself with like-minded people was my common thread to rapid success.

There is no magic bullet out there, but there are proven systems, processes and people willing to help you achieve your dreams.

The best thing anyone can do is simply believe in themselves.

Take a chance on yourself and make your own dreams become reality. We can all do it. Systems work for anybody, anywhere, at anytime.

Diamond members Rhonda Michele & Darren Salkeld with Matt Lloyd showing their 6 and 7 figure ring awards at the Titanium Mastermind Dominican Republic.

SHAQIR HUSSYIN
DIAMOND MEMBER - LONDON, UK

It's truly life changing when you go from being frustrated, confused and feeling powerless to being able to generate more money in a single day or a month than what most people would make in an entire year all thanks to the power of this system. My best day with this system has been over $55,000 and my best month has been over $155,000 in commissions. The main traffic source that I've used to attract top tier clients on autopilot is by utilising Solo Ads.

Diamond member Shaqir Hussyin receiving his 7-figure award, a 37 diamond encrusted platinum ring, at the Platinum Mastermind in Curaçao.

Get access to the ultimate HTAM (High Ticket Affiliate Marketing) system, which pays you up to $13,500 per sale at **www.fivefigureaffiliatemarketing.com**. You will also be assigned a personal HTAM coach, who will walk you through a simple, 21 step training program that shows you how to get started.

JOHN CHOW
DIAMOND MEMBER - VANCOUVER, CANADA

John Chow comes from humble beginnings, growing up in a small farming village in China with no electricity or running water. After moving to Vancouver, Canada, he got his first job at a McDonald's and lasted four hours before he quit. He worked two jobs after that, but only lasted eight months before he realized that working for someone else sucks, and never did it again.

"It's not that I'm unemployed, I'm just unemployable," says John.

When he came to terms with this, he realized the only way he could be happy working was to work for himself. After trying a few businesses, John got involved in Internet marketing and never looked back.

John has already made over $1,784,115.73 in commissions with MOBE. Shortly after joining MOBE, he had earned enough points to qualify for the MOBE Merc program. "I come from a financial planning background, so I have a personal problem with spending over $100,000 on a sports car, especially because it's technically a depreciating asset," he says. "But when Matt told me he was going to pay for my new Mercedes, I realized I'd finally get to cross the sports car off of my bucket list."

Diamond member John Chow was the first to qualify and receive a MOBE Motors. His first MOBE Motors was a white 2013 Mercedes-Benz SL550 Hardtop Convertible.

Two years later, Matt Lloyd expanded the MOBE Mercedes program to MOBE Motors (where affiliates could get all different makes of a vehicle), and John was ready to upgrade. Now he's behind the wheel of a 2015 Jaguar F-Type. "This is like having a childhood dream come true. There's nothing better than this...top down, cruising on a sunny day. And the best thing is, I don't have to pay a dime for it."

"Internet marketing has completely changed my life. I walk my daughter to school and spend the day at home with my wife every day. It's about more than money. Today, I have time, money and location freedom. I won't sugarcoat it, it requires work and a major commitment, but if you do it you can live the Dotcom lifestyle too."

. . . .

SAJ P.
DIAMOND MEMBER - LONDON, UK

I have been a full time internet marketer now for over 10 years and have made millions of dollars in that time. I have coached over 400,000 people, spoken all over the world, and have had 9 Clickbank number 1 best selling products.

I recently joined up with MOBE as an affiliate, as I believe in the company and their products and the vision of the founder Matt Lloyd. He really over delivers with everything he is doing.

I have only been promoting MOBE for a couple of months part time on the side, and in that time have generated close to $250,000 in revenue without even trying. The high ticket autopilot sales system Matt has designed is incredible and it works very well. Regardless if you are a newbie, or a seasoned pro, you can leverage the system Matt has built to create incredible income very quickly.

PAUL LYNCH
DIAMOND MEMBER - LONDON, UK

In my best day leveraging Matt's HTAM system, I've made over $29,000. My best month has been over $140,000. And so far, in the several years I've been doing this, I've made over $2 million. My results of course are not even remotely typical. I'm a seasoned internet marketing pro… and have been doing this for close to a decade now.

I actually got into this industry after sustaining an injury, which ruined my hopes of being a professional football player.

I was literally laying in a bed in hospital, looking for ways I'd be able to generate an income if I wasn't going to play football, and that's when I heard about affiliate marketing.

I started promoting peoples products, making a little money here and there. What I love about Matt's system is that for the same amount of work, I'm able to make much bigger commissions - right up to over $10,000 per sale on some of their bigger packages.

Diamond member Paul Lynch with his MOBE Motors, a Range Rover Sport, one of his dream cars since he was a teenager.

I've never seen anything else out there like it. My advice is that if you're looking at this, thinking, "I could never do that" then you need to seriously reconsider listening to that little voice. You can do this, you just need to stop making excuses, take action like I did, and work hard. You get paid to promote your links, so make sure you keep promoting. Find one traffic method, and keep practicing till you're good at it.

. . . .

RHONDA MICHELE
DIAMOND MEMBER - WINNIPEG, CANADA

My name is Rhonda Michele from Winnipeg Canada.

I've been a part of MOBE for approximately 15 months now. I immediately got positioned at the highest level, which is Diamond, in order to leverage my efforts in the best way possible.

I come from a Corporate background where I worked as a Human Resources Manager in a professional office for over 25 years. Although my career was challenging, rewarding and lucrative, it was also very demanding and stressful.

Diamond member Rhonda Michele (left) chatting with MaryEllen Tribby, one of the speakers at the Platinum Mastermind in Curaçao.

I love working directly with people on a daily basis and wanted to continue on that path. MOBE offers me the ability to interact with like-minded entrepreneurs, but now I get to do it on my own flexible schedule AND while traveling the world meeting people from all types of backgrounds!

This business allows me the ability to enjoy time freedom while making more than a full time income from my laptop — all while helping other people achieve their own goals and dreams.

To date I've been paid over $546,455.74 in commissions from the MOBE partner program, with my best day generating over $40,000.

Never let others define who you are or what you should be. Just because others have given up on their dream does not mean you need to give up on yours.

. . . .

LUKE LIM
DIAMOND MEMBER - SINGAPORE

Hi, my name is Luke Lim. I'm from Singapore, and I'm a diamond member in MOBE.

My traffic comes from PPV promoting MTTB, and from a joint venture with a business partner, Adeline, driving Facebook PPC to IM Freedom Workshop.

I have generated over half a million in commissions in a little over 2 years.

In my best month, I've made $61,712.55 and in my best day, I've made $27,085.34.

That seemed so unreal to me back then, and I started believing this whole internet marketing stuff actually works.

Prior to joining MOBE, I had been struggling in internet marketing, spending over $50,000 in 2 years buying all kinds of programs, implementing the strategies taught by the gurus but not having any results at all.

Even though I was in debt, I decided to join MOBE because I saw the potential in this system.

I borrowed money from my mother to get started in MOBE part time, while still working in a full time job as an engineer.

1 year later, I handed in my resignation letter and I've now quit my full time job.

By leveraging on what I've learned from MOBE and the connections I've built in their mastermind event, I've built my own business and scaled it up to 6 figure per month in 5 months, implementing the business strategies I've learned from MOBE.

Diamond member Luke Lim filming videos for a co-branded funnel with Matt Lloyd at the Diamond Mastermind in Bali.

• • • • • • • • • • • • • • • •

CAROLINA MILLAN
DIAMOND MEMBER - CHILE, SOUTH AMERICA

I'm Carolina Millan from Chile. I'm a Diamond Partner in MOBE. I started working with Matt Lloyd back in 2012, when the company was just beginning to gain momentum. The main traffic strategies I've been using to promote MOBE are Facebook ads and Youtube Videos.

To this date I've made half a million dollars in commissions with MOBE, something I couldn't have predicted back in 2012.

On my best day I made $20,000 dollars in commissions, and in my best month I made $29,880

Before MOBE I was working as a Social Media and Digital Marketing Consultant and also as an Independent Headhunter. I was a partner in a small Digital Marketing Agency here in Chile. I was enjoying what I was doing, but our revenue wasn't very high and I was working very hard for a $1,200 dollar

Diamond member Carolina Millan with her partner enjoying the sunshine at the MOBE Leader's Cruise, One of the awards for affiliates that exceed $100,000 in commissions.

cheque. When things with MOBE started to take off I told my partners I would step aside and start doing something that would give me more money and location freedom. Working with local clients was very time consuming and required me to be at meetings every week.

Thanks to my success in MOBE I was able to branch out and start offering my own products and services to people around the World. I'm very passionate about helping others discover the possibilities the internet has for them.

The same year I started with MOBE things were very uncertain. I was barely making ends meet, my boyfriend had also quit his job and we had just started to pay a mortgage for our new apartment. That same year my mother was diagnosed with a liver tumor, and my dad was about to retire. So I knew things HAD to work, because I wanted to help my family.

I wasn't new to IM, but MOBE was the first time I ever made a dollar online. I had been struggling since 2008 when I was brand new and still had a job in human resources. I invested thousands in courses and joined an MLM company, but nothing really worked for me, I didn't have the mindset and the right direction.

I still remember when I made my first $100 dollars with MOBE. It was in March 2012 and I had just started a campaign with Bing Ads as my coach at the time told me to. I didn't know what I was doing, but logging in to my back office and seeing those $100 dollars sitting there made me realise it was all worth it. I knew from that moment on I would be unstoppable.

If you're wondering, my mom is doing great, I've been able to finance her natural treatments (I buy supplements online for her every month so she can stay healthy). And I'm glad to be able to help my dad with his bills too.

I get to travel the World, speak on stages and mastermind with very successful people. I feel very grateful for what I've achieved. If a girl from Chile could do this, I don't see why anyone else couldn't!

I'm excited to see how far MOBE will go in the Online Education Industry.

· · · · · · · · · · · · · · ·

CHRIS COBB
DIAMOND MEMBER - LONDON, UNITED KINGDOM

My name is Chris Cobb and I am from the UK. Before I started with MOBE I was already a full-time Internet Marketer, but MOBE has given me a new lease of life in terms of setting goals, striving for the next level and stretching my thinking. What I've learned from the events in the last year alone has been nothing short of phenomenal and I'm looking forward to learning more and networking with affiliates for years to come.

I've made millions online and it just shows that you should never stop learning and always plug yourself into the right systems, work with the right people and set new goals.

I first started out of frustration as I was fed up with my corporate job and I had also built up a reasonably large personal debt as well which prompted me to change what I was doing with my life. I funded my first business using nothing but credit cards and have never looked back. It was one of the scariest things

Diamond member Chris Cobb with his first and second MOBE Motors, an Audi Q5 and a Range Rover Sports, one of his childhood dream cars.

I've ever done looking back and the advice that I received at the time was NOT to tell anyone. Just get on and do it and let others ask questions when you've made it and they wonder how you did it.

So far I have made over $442,019.28 with MOBE including prize money. My best day has been over $18,000 and my best month $73,160.98.

· · · · · · · · · · · · · · · · · ·

DAVID GILKS
DIAMOND MEMBER - PERTH, AUSTRALIA

I'm David Gilks, a Diamond affiliate of MOBE from Perth, Australia. I've now made $253,340 USD from my online business.

Before starting my online business my profession was a software engineer and I worked for banks, universities and other large companies. My skills didn't translate to an entrepreneurial business so I had a lot to learn and implement by using the MOBE training and attending the mastermind events.

In my best day I've had a $10,000 commission and my best week so far has been $17,000 in commissions. I don't make this sort of money every day, or every week, but I can comfortably work from home building my business and consultancy.

Diamond member David Gilks enjoying the sunset at the Diamond Mastermind in Bali

What I really love is the lifestyle freedom an online business provides. I can be home to take my son to school and pick him up at the end of the day. I certainly don't miss the long commute to the city each day; a 30 second walk to my home office suites me just fine!

Get access to the ultimate HTAM (High Ticket Affiliate Marketing) system, which pays you up to $13,500 per sale at **www.fivefigureaffiliatemarketing.com**. You will also be assigned a personal HTAM coach, who will walk you through a simple, 21 step training program that shows you how to get started.

· · · · · · · · · · · · · · · ·

ADELINE SUGIANTO
DIAMOND MEMBER - SYDNEY, AUSTRALIA

My name is Adeline Sugianto, a MOBE Diamond Member from Sydney, Australia. In less than 2 years, I have generated a total of $312,485.79 in commissions primarily through Facebook Paid Per Click promoting MOBE Live Events.

My best month has been $33,175.23 so far in MOBE and I've made as much as $15,200 in a single day - which is more than what I've made in my full-time job in a month working day and night!

Before MOBE, I was working as a full-time solar cell engineer. I planned to work very hard to climb up the corporate ladder and double my salary if I maintain an exceptional performance until one day I lost my job! It was not easy to get a new job afterwards and that was an awakening moment for me that I was not going to depend on anyone else for my own financial future. I felt frustrated, desperate and alone but I knew this was only going to bring a good change.

I started looking into different ways of earning income and I stumbled upon Internet Marketing. I just fell in love with the potential of being able to work anywhere around the world with just a laptop and internet connection. I could immediately sense freedom, independence and limitlessness.

I started from scratch, with no prior experience and no list/following/connections in the industry. I did not even dare to tell that I was doing this to my family because they would definitely think I was entering some Ponzi scheme. They thought I was being scammed and advised me to be careful and not invest a chunk of my hard earned money into the business.

Sadly, a lot of my friends and family did not believe in me because the 'A' s and 'B's were typically employed by the 'C's and 'D's... the academias will not make it when it comes to running their own business successfully.

But I knew that this is what I wanted to do. Even when I did not have enough cash to invest, I found a way because I would do everything it took to succeed.

Real entrepreneurs are resourceful. I applied for a 1-year interest-free credit card to fund my Titanium and Platinum investment to 6 different banks and after a few rounds of interviews and rejections, finally 2 of them approved my applications!

In 5 months, I made my Platinum investment back and generated over $1 million dollar in sales ever since.

Diamond member Adeline Sugianto filming her branding videos at the Diamond Mastermind in Bali.

· · · · · · · · · · · · · · · · · ·

PAUL O'MAHONY
DIAMOND MEMBER - GALWAY, IRELAND

In July of 2015, I had a pay day of over $100,000 from exactly 90 minutes work and best of all, it wasn't my work! Not only that, with the follow up that number doubled within 6 weeks!

How did I do this?

I have a friend who runs events for business owners. I asked him if there was an availability to have a speaker from MOBE to deliver an overview of the system and make them an irresistible offer. That is exactly what happened.

This is something that anyone can do provided you know people who run events of any size related to business of any kind.

MOBE is an incredible system. Where else can you provide real and practical solutions to business owners in terms of how to grow their brand and presence online and get paid to have the worlds' leading experts deliver the training for you?

Diamond member Paul O'Mahony enjoying his brand new MOBE Motors.

· · · · · · · · · · · · · · · · · ·

ANDREA GOODSAID
DIAMOND MEMBER - FLORIDA, USA

My name is Andrea Goodsaid. I am a stay-at-home mom with 3 wonderful children that I love very much. I love my husband too, but he was not supportive of affiliate marketing when I got started. He quickly changed his mind when he saw the large commissions coming in though! To date, I've earned $190,563 through the MOBE High Ticket Affiliate Program and I'm making more now in less time than I ever did before.

When I started with affiliate marketing, my husband John was my worst critic. Probably the worst barbs were the ones about me "yacking" all day online not getting anything done. Then everything changed when I started making large commissions through MOBE's high ticket affiliate marketing program. The big commissions made it legitimate in his eyes. Today, I put in a lot less time, but my income per sale has gone way up. The MOBE High Ticket Affiliate Program has been a true blessing for my family and me.

Diamond member Andrea Goodsaid revealing her co-branded eBook with Matt Lloyd at the Diamond Mastermind Cancun.

Get access to the ultimate HTAM (High Ticket Affiliate Marketing) system, which pays you up to $13,500 per sale at **www.fivefigureaffiliatemarketing.com**. You will also be assigned a personal HTAM coach, who will walk you through a simple, 21 step training program that shows you how to get started.

· · · · · · · · · · · · · ·

GEORG KERSCHHACKL
DIAMOND MEMBER - VERONA, ITALY

Georg Kerschhackl is a Diamond member from Verona, Italy. He spent 30 years working first in a government job and later in the insurance industry when he started to feel tired and lacked job satisfaction. When his youngest son got diagnosed with a rare disease, he knew something had to change.

"I wanted to design a life for myself that would allow me to spend precious time with my family" said George.

"That's when I discovered MOBE. MOBE's done-for-you systems gave me the freedom to work from my laptop, anywhere I had an internet connection. It gave me back the family time that I needed to be with my sons."

So far Georg has made over $176,436.14 with MOBE, with his best day being $11,086.03 and his best month $22,702.05. His main method of traffic is retargeting.

Diamond member Georg Kerschhackl enjoying more time with his family and a brand new MOBE Motors Maserati

······················

TERRY LAMB
DIAMOND MEMBER - FORT LAUDERDALE, FLORIDA

My name is Terry Lamb and have been I was in affiliate marketing for years making small commissions but when I found MOBE the $1,250 commissions were a game changer and then I became aware of the $3,300 and $5,500 commissions and generating income at those levels made my entire online business so much easier to profit from.

After many years of pay cuts in the airline industry (I was a Captain for a major US airline) I simply couldn't take it any longer, years of college and training only to have my income cut and my future retirement drained away? I knew that getting an online education was the answer, I had seen other success stories of regular everyday people and I knew I could duplicate their success, I just needed the right vehicle so to speak and MOBE was that vehicle.

My internet marketing method to build my online business was simple, create a short video for YouTube expressing the power of the MOBE system (without

Diamond member Terry Lamb adding more commissions to his affiliate marketing business; seen here at the Super Charge Summit Las Vegas

Get access to the ultimate HTAM (High Ticket Affiliate Marketing) system, which pays you up to $13,500 per sale at www.fivefigureaffiliatemarketing.com. You will also be assigned a personal HTAM coach, who will walk you through a simple, 21 step training program that shows you how to get started.

mentioning it specifically) and asking interested viewers to call me to learn more and in my first week I earned $58,000 in commissions with the MOBE license rights program.

With MOBE as my "vehicle" for profits and consistent income stream I am able to travel 10+ times per year, have complete freedom in my life and never have to look back toward a "job" as a way to create income . I can now leverage the MOBE system and earn the income I need to live the lifestyle I deserve; freedom is easy if you have the education and tools that MOBE provides, all you have to do is leverage them as I have.

So far, my best month with MOBE has been $89,000 and my best day $14,000.

· · · · · · · · · · · · · · · · · ·

VIKAS KUMRAI
DIAMOND MEMBER - PUNJAB, INDIA

Hi, this is Vikas KumRai, a MOBE Diamond member from Punjab, a northern state in India. This business has given me immense wealth in such a short span and it has been a life-changer for me. I have earned over $93,755.37 with MOBE in less than 2 years. MOBE has earned me 9k on a particular day. My highest monthly earning in MOBE stands at 22k. These are enormous figures removing any suspicion around an internet marketing business.

My journey with Internet Marketing started just 2 years back. Before that, I was a regular employee of Walmart and doing only a regular 9 to 6 job. I used to earn $700 a month. It was a life full of limitations only: *"you can't do this"*, *"you can't do that"*... and you even stop dreaming big.

However, on one lucky day I lost my job. I call it a lucky day because otherwise I would still be doing the same old job. I can't thank my boss enough for firing me.

You realize your true potential when you are completely cornered and my job loss just did the same to me. I had a little bit of experience in internet marketing earlier but I got myself involved full-time after loosing my job. I started with MLR the basic level and closed my first sale over my 1st ever call in less than a week.

That $1,200 commission day was a big moment. The Law of money is "*Money Attracts Money*", but I didn't have money to play big, so I borrowed. I reached the diamond level with the borrowed money and there has not been a single day of regret.

For a newbie in Internet marketing, there couldn't be a better system than MOBE. For any new business, you need to take care of hundreds of things - capital, manpower, products, training, sales and so many things. Here, MOBE takes care of all your worries. You just have to take care of the initial capital. My earnings in such a short span couldn't have been possible in any other system but MOBE.

Today, I consider myself financially independent. It gives a different meaning to life when you achieve your financial freedom. Life has become so much wonderful. I couldn't thank MOBE enough.

Diamond member Vikas KumRai receiving his award of excellence at the Platinum Mastermind in Kota Kinabalu, Malaysia.

CHAN AIK HOON
DIAMOND MEMBER - SINGAPORE

I am Chan Aik Hoon, a baby boomer from Singapore. My first job was in nursing. I specialized in nursing patients after their open-heart surgery in the intensive care unit. In the 70s, I had the privilege of nursing the first few hundreds of heart by-pass surgical patients. I also counseled the depressed and suicidal. Juggling these two was a very challenging task so I decided to leave the hospital for the Direct Sales/MLM (multi-level marketing) industry, which would give me the flexibility of time to care for the depressed and rescue them from suicide attempts.

In 2009, I traveled extensively in the region to expand my MLM business. A virus attacked my lungs and I almost died. For 3 years, I was very ill. I couldn't work as I was short of breath every single day. My recovery was painfully

Diamond member Chan Aik Hoon with Matt Lloyd at the Super Charge Summit Singapore

long and slow. I knew I couldn't return to MLM. I often wondered if there was another option for me.

I was introduced to Internet marketing (IM), which I knew nothing about but I was fascinated. I explored and bought many IM programs. Then, I met Matt Lloyd in person in February of 2012 and bought his newly launched MLR program. As I was still ill, I didn't do anything with it until he launched the Titanium & Platinum Mastermind events, and also the Free MOBE Merc Incentive in 2013. The latter caught my attention, as I live in Singapore and a Mercedes here would cost S$300,000. I gave up driving in March 2013 so it would be a big deal for me to get a Free MOBE car in Singapore!

After completing the MTTB 21 Steps, I knew MOBE was my other option. Because of my Cardiac Intensive Care Training I valued high-quality stuff. To me, MOBE is that high-quality stuff for IM industry. In business, you want to maximize your profits. So, I became fully positioned in Titanium & Platinum. As my health improved further, in the first week of January 2014, over a 4 day period, I closed 2 sales and earned USD $30,488.20! Not bad for someone brand new in IM. Only MOBE could have given me this kind of opportunity.

How did I achieve these results? Well, I work on what I know and do best (i.e. warm markets.) With my 20 years of MLM experience, I love working with warm markets and I'm confident closing my own sales and doing phone follow-ups. In my MOBE business, I worked much less than I did in the MLM business. So far I have earned a total of USD $144,385.34 and the most exciting thing is I became the first person in Singapore and Asia to own a FREE MOBE Motor Car!

So, if you're reading this book right now, you're looking for another option, you could be a baby boomer, approaching retirement or may already be retired, wherever you are located (especially in Singapore where cars are 5 times more expensive than in USA), or if you've got no prior experience in Internet marketing like myself, I encourage you to take look at MOBE. I look forward to working with you and helping you make money online.

ALWYN & CAROL MONTEIRO
DIAMOND MEMBERS - TORONTO, CANADA

Diamond Member Alwyn Monteiro from Toronto, Canada spent 24 years working on his career, but after 3 layoffs, he knew a job was far from stable and wanted to do something more that he could be in total control of.

Alwyn and his wife Carol were always planners and knew what they wanted, which was :

♦ Retire in a tropical country long before the age of 65

♦ Travel more and explore new cultures

♦ Live a life of adventure

Making a switch from an employee to an entrepreneur happened in stages for Alwyn. With Carol's encouragement, his first transformational step was to quit his full time job and start his own consulting practice. This was the beginning of a mindset shift for both of them as they started their journey into entrepreneurship.

Diamond members Alwyn and Carol Monteiro with their Porsche Cayenne MOBE Motors

However after long hours and high stress as a consultant, something needed to change and Alwyn's search led him to business opportunities online. That is where Alwyn found MOBE.

MOBE offered Alwyn & Carol all they desired i.e. the freedom to work from anywhere and to live the life they had envisioned. The journey got even more exciting when Carol attended her first MOBE Mastermind and was fully on board with the idea.

Together they decided to position themselves as Diamond Members and take advantage of the high ticket commissions.

Today they use Social Media to grow their network and email list e.g. Twitter, Facebook and Periscope and local meet-ups.

Their best day with MOBE was $8,000. To date, the training they received through MOBE has also allowed them to earn over $265,000 completely unrelated to MOBE. The training they received at MOBE has helped their other businesses significantly.

. . . .

DAVID MITCHELL
DIAMOND MEMBER - VICTORIA, AUSTRALIA

My name is David Mitchell and I am 66 years of age. I live with my wife Jill in Wandin, the Yarra Valley (just outside Melbourne, Victoria, Australia.)

I am a MOBE Diamond Member, and my main traffic method is Facebook PPC promoting live events. I am following Adeline Sugianto's methods.

So far, I have made just over $21,024 through MOBE. The biggest day to me was when I made my first $1000. Tears were streaming down my face. I now knew this would work. That lead to my best day of $4000 – the same month total was $8049.

I came from a background of land surveying and GIS. Some years ago, I couldn't work for a long period because of ill-health. To get back into employment I took a casual job in public transport. Early in 2014, I had been in that job for nearly nine years. Many hours were unpaid time and two to five hours were spent travelling each day. The work was mind numbing. Frustration and disappointment were constant companions. I was going downhill financially, physically, spiritually and emotionally. I had been applying for other vacancies but, at my age, a new position was hard to come by.

I had been stagnating for far too long. I did not want to be on a long slide any longer. I needed to be free to move ahead. I decided to take the bull by the horns: I resigned from my job. I was only a casual employee, so, one day's notice was enough.

I spent the next six months searching for something to do for a living – even for a future career. I needed something that would be time and place flexible. I had family spread all over the country that I wanted to keep closer contact with. I knew it would be on the internet that I would find the key – but what?

I looked at online stores and blogs. I found myself starting to follow examples of the weird and wonderful presenters on YouTube. I am sure some of the

Diamond member David Mitchell taking notes at the Platinum Mastermind Kota Kinabalu, Malaysia.

ideas in the videos worked, others, well...? I studied quite a few YouTube videos by internet marketers. While some made sense others they were years out of date and no longer relevant. The methods they used no longer provided the results of earlier times.

Some people have offers out there to make money internet marketing. Some of them were a little dodgy. I am not saying they were scams – I just did not know. I stayed clear of these.

I decided to look into internet marketing in more detail. It made sense. I found other videos with presenters talking about top tier products. I liked Matt Lloyd's MOBE videos. I needed my products already created, no customer support responsibilities, no handling payments, no doing it on my own.

Remember, I was a complete newbie in running any business on the Internet. I had used computers since the 1960's but nothing for serious commerce at all. Matt's system looked solid and exciting. It was what I was after.

I read about the Home Business Summit to be held in Sydney. It was being presented by MOBE. I decided to go to learn more and meet the people involved. After my ticket purchase went through, I was given the opportunity to enroll in MTTB. I soon realised MOBE is a solid organisation with a sustainable business plan. That weekend I got positioned at the Platinum level.

. . . .

BRANDON ODOM
PLATINUM MEMBER - SIERRA VISTA, ARIZONA

I'm Brandon Odom and I've earned $20,036.51 in commissions as a Platinum member in MOBE. I got started with MTTB in April of 2015 and started promoting MOBE in May. I focused on running Facebook ads promoting MOBE live events.

My best day in MOBE so far came in July 2015 when I made $10,050 in a single day because of a sale at a live event I promoted. It felt really good to get that sale because I felt validated that I made the right decision to move forward with my business. A decision that was pretty risky for me at the time.

I'm a former US Army officer from Arkansas who lives in Arizona, and after leaving the military, I became a full-time entrepreneur and real estate investor. My properties cash-flowed but my business ventures didn't. At the same time I was starting in MOBE, I found out I had lost $100,000+ in a business investment that turned out to be fraudulent. At the time of this book's publication I'm still in a lawsuit trying to recoup some of those losses. Additionally, years of relationship strain from military deployments and duty location separations, the financial stress of our financial losses, and poor priorities on my part caused my relationship with my wife to deteriorate. I found myself literally homeless for almost a month. It was during that time I lived out of my 15-year old truck and worked out of coffee shops to build my business.

I cashed out all my investments in the market and invested into positioning in MOBE and to pay for advertising. I figured the best investment I could make was in my online marketing education and my own business, rather than someone else's business.

Platinum member Brandon Odom next to his MOBE Motors, Chevrolet Colorado.

What I learned from MOBE allowed me to become successful marketing several other products online, earn thousands of dollars in commissions and sustain myself as a full-time internet marketer.

I qualified for the MOBE Motors program and got a new truck (and I didn't have to live out of it thankfully). Over the rest of the year my wife and I reconciled and I also began building a conventional business following my passion for dancing while working with some other products online. I now teach Latin dancing part-time and also host a dance night at a venue in town and what I've learned about building a list, copywriting, Facebook advertising and business in general through MOBE this last year has helped me to dominate my market in Phoenix.

Now that I have some stability I'm once again shifting focus back to MOBE with a goal to become a 7-figure earner within the next 2 years.

- - - - - - - - - - - - - - - - -

NAVJOT SINGH
MLR MEMBER - PUNJAB, INDIA

Hi my name is Navjot Singh, a Pharmacist from Punjab, INDIA.

After working for more than 7 years, I realized that I did not love my job, which had minimal opportunity for growth. I did not love the long working hours that included a lot of responsibilities and what I considered to be a low salary. So, I started looking for some opportunities over the Internet, which could help me make money, and one day, from an online ad, I learned about MOBE and decided to join.

I never made so much commission online with any affiliate program before. To date, I have earned $60,997.03 with $1,617 on my best day and $6,232 in my best month. My main source of traffic is PPC and Blogging.

When my father used to see me working on my computer, he would always say to me that you can't make money online, and that I was just wasting my time and money. He believed that what I'm doing is "not real work". Basically, he never showed support for my online business.

But, my mother and wife always supported my online business. Most importantly, they gave me money that allowed me to get a credit card, so I can pay $1,997 for MOBE License Rights.

Learn from my story – you may struggle to put in the time and effort, but if you implement and don't quit, you will see great things happen in your business and your life.

. . . .

YANNICK VAN DEN BOS
DIAMOND MEMBER - PLAYA DEL CARMEN, MEXICO

My name is Yannick van den Bos and I am originally from the Netherlands, but honestly I have no country that I really call home. The world is my playground.

Thanks to HTAM (High-Ticket Affiliate Marketing) I've been able to live a life of total freedom. Living in places like Johannesburg (South Africa), Shanghai (China), Phuket (Thailand) and now in tropical Playa del Carmen (Mexico).

I also was able to fly my mother out to Riviera, Mexico for an all paid vacation where I surprised her with a check paying off all her financial debt.

Since joining MOBE, I've been able to earn over $178,933.71 in paid commissions. I started promoting MOBE and it's HTAM model through my personal blog, Facebook and YouTube channel.

Once those automated systems were in place I shifted into promoting the live events through direct response advertising.

Live events really is where my passion is, because these free preview workshops really touch peoples lives and impact them in a positive way.

It's for that reason that I now travel with the events team, where I'm able to share my success with MOBE and inspire people who want to get started with this HTAM success model.

Limitless has shown you what's possible and I'm living proof that this HTAM success model works.

Whatever decision you choose to make, always remember that you will always know that you were one of the first people worldwide to get this *Limitless* book which will help you create the lifestyle of your dreams.

The only difference is what you choose to do with that knowledge. You are destined for greatness; so don't settle for average.

Apply the action steps that you read in this book consistently, and I promise you that your life will drastically change, as it did for me.

Diamond member Yannick van den Bos with his 6-figure award, a 16 diamond encrusted platinum ring, awarded to MOBE affiliates who cross over $100K in commissions. Seen here at the Titanium Mastermind Dominican Republic.

SUSAN GEER ZANGI

DIAMOND MEMBER - CHARLOTTE, NORTH CAROLINA

My name is Susan Geer Zanghi and I found MOBE one day when, feeling completely frustrated, unappreciated, and unstable in my current job, I clicked on a link from an advertisement promoting a work from home opportunity. I was looking for the time freedom that a work from home job allows.

I was building my MOBE business on the side while still in my corporate job when I got the news that my current position was being eliminated due to downsizing. As luck would have it, 2 days later, I received an email advertising a position working as Matt Lloyd's personal executive assistant. I jumped at the chance to work along side this brilliant young man - and I have never looked back.

In less that one year, I earned $20,755.13 through the MOBE high ticket affiliate program - all while working full time for Matt and doing a minimal amount of work on my home business. I know that the system works and that I can increase what I have already achieved if I follow the directions of Matt Lloyd and the MOBE team. So far my biggest payday was a $3,000 on May 27 2015 and my biggest month was $3264.60 in May 2015.

Diamond member Susan Geer Zanghi talking with Matt Lloyd and Diamond member Russell Whitney at the Platinum Mastermind Fiji

· · · · · · · · · · · · · · · · · ·

RON & RHONDA KEENAN
DIAMOND MEMBERS - UMINA BEACH, NEW SOUTH WALES

We joined this business in March of 2015. The very next month April we jumped out of the gate and made a handsome $1,120 commission. Then in May we were really on fire and made $14,200 commissions $14,000 of that was in 1 day.

In June we kept rolling along and made a further $1,349.50. July $5,149.50 and so it just keeps going along with sales reaching $54,725.00.

All of this was done without advertising. Just spreading the word and talking to people on this great company and showing others how they can change their lives. It is possible & you can do it too.

Diamond members Ron & Rhonda Keenan celebrating their 40th wedding anniversary at the Titanium Mastermind Welcome Dinner in Phuket, Thailand

If you'd like to get more daily inspirational stories like these
(which will help keep you focused on achieving your own goals in MOBE),
go to **www.mobeinspiration.com.**

Email Examples

Your email list will be one of your most valuable assets. As you start and grow your business focus on building and growing your list. To get real and scalable results you will need to keep your list engaged and learn how to write profit-pulling emails.

Below are some of examples of my personal emails. Notice how I use everyday stories and turn them into call to actions. You can do the same.

EMAIL EXAMPLE 1

Subject: 240k spent in last 12 months on books, courses, and seminars (and why)

Hey,

So right now I'm at high end business Conference here in Fort Lauderdale, Florida. It's not my conference, but I was asked to speak today about the growth of MOBE, and how we have scaled so quickly.

Most people were fascinated to hear about it, because of how it's grown so quickly yet is an almost entirely virtual organisation.

I actually traveled 32 hours just to attend this conference a few days ago, and head back home (well, actually I head to Sydney for another event, and then home) tomorrow.

While sitting in the audience today, I was reflecting on how much money I've spent on my own education over the past 12 months.

I calculated it to be well over $240,000, (which even surprised me!).

A few years ago, I would have balked at spending that kind of money on consulting, going to seminars, and buying info-products.

I would have thought it was ridiculous.

But these days, I know that getting the right information from the right sources, is about the most important thing I can do.

The right information when applied, can be (and has been) worth millions of dollars.

After I get this information and then implement it and verify it works, I then strive to share it with YOU through our live mastermind seminars.

Unfortunately though, not everyone can always attend these.

For some, the investment is out of their reach - the minimum entry fee is $10,000, and they are held in exotic countries all around the world (like Fiji, Bahamas, Thailand, etc) that not everyone can travel to.

So the next best way to get access to some of this high level information, is through my monthly print newsletters.

I send these newsletters right to your doorstep every 30 days if you become a paid subscriber.

And the January issue is about to go out in the next 48 hours.

Get access to the ultimate HTAM (High Ticket Affiliate Marketing) system, which pays you up to $13,500 per sale at **www.fivefigureaffiliatemarketing.com**. You will also be assigned a personal HTAM coach, who will walk you through a simple, 21 step training program that shows you how to get started.

The good news is, for a very limited time you can get the first issue of each of these newsletters for FREE, so long as you help out with shipping and handling - which is just a few bucks.

The most high-end of these Inner Circle newsletters, (Platinum), normally sells for $299 / month. But you can get it for free today if you take action.

Here's what is covered in each one (my recommendation is to get the Platinum because it contains the other 2 newsletters with it):

Gold Inner Circle (for beginner marketers):

In this month's issue you'll learn:

* Why a little expensive coaching beats a flood of cheap advice when it comes to growing your business

* How the 'no-money' excuse compromises the seller, and why the best sales people, marketers and stage presenters reject this pitiful excuse outright

* 12 Laws of Life' that you can use to turn entrepreneurial hell into paradise

* 4 ways to combat the loneliness of home-based entrepreneurship

* Why a series of "little moments" can create a great experience for your customers and keep them coming back

* How creating a customer avatar will inform your content and grow your business

Grow your business with our Gold Inner Circle...

Titanium Inner Circle
(for intermediate - advanced marketers):

In this month's issue you'll learn:

* The right way to hire a CFO

* How to land your best clients through public speaking

- Essential ingredients for crafting an irresistible call-to-action

- 5 go-to conversion optimization tools

- Tips and tricks for relaxing your sales prospect

Leverage Traffic and Marketing Strategies with Titanium...

Platinum Inner Circle (for entrepreneurs who want to increase their wealth through investing):

In this month's issue you'll learn:

- Why putting a system of checks and balances in place is the best thing you can do to keep your honest employees honest—and eliminate temptation

- How to squeeze the maximum yield from every asset you own

- Next steps on the journey from $0 to $17K/month in 12 months

- 5 hidden costs of pessimism

- 10 rules every great speaker must follow

- 3 actionable tips for boosting mobile conversion

Learn more about our Prestigious Platinum Inner Circle... (and get the other 2 issues above included for free)

Oh, and one more thing - somewhat related...

Another guy I know who spends almost as much as me on consulting, buying courses, and investing in his knowledge is a good friend of mine, and also one of the top affiliate marketers in our industry.

For promoting MOBE over the last few years, I've paid him over $2 million. In total from all his revenue streams, he's made a lot more.

Just for my subscribers (YOU), he's going to be hosting a training workshop this Thursday at 7pm EST which you should attend.

Register Here.

His training sessions are always entertaining - they've also been known to drag on for hours, but no one ever seems to mind because there's so much value being delivered. I highly recommend you attend.

Talk soon,

Matt

.... **EMAIL EXAMPLE 2** ....

Subject: Obsession

Hey,

Right now, I'm in Bali, Indonesia checking out resorts for a future event we might host here in 2014.

I was just out at a restaurant downtown, eating crab, with a live band playing in the background.

People were dancing... smiling... having a good time all around me.

But to be completely honest with you, I was bored out of my mind.

There's probably something wrong with me.

But the truth is, most of the everyday things people love to do don't interest me.

I almost feel out of place in those surroundings.

The only place I feel fully engaged, and truly at home, is behind my computer, building and creating my business.

I love my business.

People think I'm obsessed with it. And, they're right - I am.

MOBE is not a vehicle to get me to a certain dollar figure in a year or two, and then sit back and enjoy the proceeds.

It's a life long obsession, and I am literally prepared to devote the rest of my life to it.

My favorite part of these entire business, is seeing people get results.

This is where I get my entertainment.

Not just the same old regular top affiliates either...

I like to see the new guy make a thousand buck commission, when he's never made a dollar online before.

I like to see that lady who got laid off from her teaching job, now working at McDonald's (she knows who she is) turn it all around, and start having 20 grand months with MOBE.

That's my entertainment.

I love to see people surprise themselves, because most of them are walking around in a daze, oblivious to their own awesome potential.

So to celebrate those people, I wanted to show you some videos I've got in the last few days from 3 of them.

They are not gurus.

They're just everyday people who had the balls to take a chance, get started in MOBE, and put in the work.

The first video I wanna show you, is from a fireman.

His name is Russell Armstrong. 2 days ago, he had an 8k day.

Instead of doing the usual video testimonial... he decided to surprise his family with the news and get it all on camera.

This is what he came back with:

www.mattlloyd.tv/fireman-tells-his-family

Can't help but smile when you see that...

The next guy, is a young heavy metal Swedish rocker - who's in a band, and sells his songs on itunes.

I'm not even going to tell you how much he made in 30 days, because too many people reading this wouldn't believe it.

So you'll have to let him tell you in his video - and check out the new car he got at the end (which MOBE is paying for):

www.mattlloyd.tv/rob-paris-35k-and-a-free-mercedes

That's gotta be one of my new favorites.

And then lastly, is another one of the many people who get started in MOBE, have been trying to make this online business work for years, and have never really hit it big.

Well, this guy finally did.

I called him at 1am Sydney time (he was still up) and interviewed him on skype, asking how he did it. Take a look:

www.mattlloyd.tv/earnie-makes-8k

What I like most about Ernie, is he told me he's been at this for years. When persistence pays off, there's no better feeling.

Anyway... I just wanted to share those stories with you.

Maybe you'll get some inspiration from them.

Maybe you're still working hard at this, not getting the results you want... but, this will help show you that you can do this.

These are the kind of people I've asked to come speak at our next live event, in Arizona, December 13th-15th.

I'm purposely making the focus of our next live all about the 'regular joes' who are getting results, and asking them to share how they're doing it.

If you're interested in coming, here's the details:
www.SuperChargeSummit.com

And if you want to use the same system the above 3 people are using, it's **HERE**.

Talk soon,

Matt

························· **EMAIL EXAMPLE 3** ·························

Subject: The Extra '0'

Hey,

So it's been 5.5 years since I first discovered this world of online marketing.

It all started with an innocent Google search.

For my first 2 years, my results were mediocre (to put it nicely).

Basically, I'd put 40k AUD into another business (this is long before MOBE ever existed).

I was making nothing, and I had no clue what I was doing.

It took me 9 months working 12 hours a day, before I ever saw an ounce of results.

September 2009 was when I got my first 'taste' - finally, I got my first 1k commission.

I can't really describe the feeling... but I can say that when it happens for you, you'll understand why getting that first result is so vitally important.

Now you know it's possible.

And you know you can repeat those action steps again to reproduce the same result.

(you knew it was possible for other people to get results of course - but now you know it's possible for you).

Now, if you'd known me back in 2009, I was the guy you'd see at the seminars who you'd never predict would be successful.

None of this came naturally to me.

But things soon changed.

In late 2011, I got a small amount of momentum behind me; and once I had some, I made absolute sure I rode that wave for as long as I could.

Fast forward to 2014, and the company I started (MOBE) went on to produce in the multiple 8 figures for the year.

Do you know what separated me from peers in 2014, who built multiple 6 figure businesses, while I went on to ascend into the 8 figure bracket?

I was willing to take bigger bets for the bigger rewards.

It reminds me of a piece of advice I had a few years ago:

The only difference between a 100k deal, and a 1m deal, is the extra '0.'

How many zeros are you comfortable with?

In the recording you're about to watch, I will show you what it looks like to go put 1.5m of hard earned USD into traffic... and turn it into a much larger amount.

Please study this video.

So many people I talk to in our industry have no idea what the life cycle of marketing is, and getting a good ROI looks like.

So many are looking for instant results.

But this is how it looks in reality:

www.mobe.tv/1-5-million-on-traffic

I hope you get some really valuable lessons from this.

Talk soon,

Matt Lloyd

Subject: Please do not laugh at my hair cut

Hey,

So a week ago, before getting on a plane for Florida to head over for the MOBE Leaders Cruise, I walked into a trendy hairdresser salon in Kuala Lumpur and told them to give me a 'modern' haircut.

Jason (my trendy hairdresser) said, "no problem!," and proceeded to pick up an electric shaver and take off a huge chunk of my entire side section of my hair.

He literally shaved it right off!

To make things look even, he of course had to do the same exact thing on the other side!

The result was making my haircut look a little like a mushroom. Or a 2014 Justin Bieber haircut style.

For your amusement, see it here in this video on Youtube in all it's glory:

Click Here to watch.

Anyway... I'm not that bothered about it now. Even though it was a bit of a shock at first, it's growing on me.

Mainly I just wanted to get your attention and get you to watch that video, where I answer the question,

"Is there a good reason behind having a $7-10 front end offer in your business?"

In the last email I sent you, I talked about the power of positioning.

About how much easier it makes things when you are perceived as 'the guru' in your space.

A big part of the reason why people get involved in our Diamond Mastermind program (and invest 30k), is that delivers guru positioning.

The sales funnel we build for the clients includes their own self-branded ebook $10 offer (and of course, much more).

These clients can then go market the ebook, to get front-end buyers.

The $10 they make on these front-end buyers is irrelevant. It's barely going to make a dent in their advertising budget.

The real asset for them, is the customer they obtain.

That customer can be like an oil well... that keeps on pumping out new oil for years to come.

As long as the client follows up with additional offers, and provides value in the areas where their customer needs it, they can take that $10 buyer and over time turn him/her into a $50,000 buyer (and even above).

You may not believe me when you hear those kind of figures.

5 years ago, I wouldn't have believed those numbers either.

But it's true - I've seen it many, many hundreds of times in my own company.

The reason I bring all this up is because tomorrow night a good friend of mine, who I have trusted to be the main trainer at the last 2 Diamond Masterminds, is going to be putting on a training session on how YOU can become the GURU in your niche.

Whether you're an affiliate for MOBE in the IM space, or, you're marketing in some other completely different niche, what you learn on this training will still apply.

I am strongly recommending you attend. Even if that means staying up into the wee hours of the morning because you're in another time zone, you should still attend.

Out of all of our weekly webinar trainers we have, Norbert gets some of the highest feedback for value provided.

The webinar starts 9pm EST, Thursday night (tonight, depending on where you are in the world).

You can register for it here:

www.mobemarketplace.com/weekly-webinar

By the way, I am sending this email specifically to MOBE License Rights affiliates (and above) because I think that out of all the many hundreds of thousands of people on our lists... this training is particularly going to benefit you the most.

Do everything you can to make sure you attend.

Talk soon,

Matt

Subject: How to make 2016 a record revenue year (and my own personal plan)

Hey,

So right now I'm on a farm in south west Australia (my parents) for a few days... our nearest local town (5 minutes away) has a population of about 15 people.

The days between Christmas and New Years are where I like to do a lot of deep thinking about the future, and since the farm here is one of the quietest places on earth, it's where I like to spend this time.

I've been planning out 2016. Major, major changes are coming. Good changes. You'll hear about these soon.

As for our revenue target (and our 'commissions paid to affiliates' target) I have enormous goals.

I'd like to triple what we did in 2015. It's not going to be easy, but it's doable.

If I'm being completely honest with you (and I don't like admitting this), exactly 12 months ago I sat on this same chair at our kitchen table, making equally ambitious goals.

Here I am one year later, and I have fallen short of achieving those goals.

Don't get me wrong; 2015 was still a record year for MOBE, where we more than doubled what we did in 2014.

But I failed to meet my targets.

So I've been reflecting a lot of why.

Why did I not hit those targets (and why do so many others not hit their targets?)

The answer is simple.

I did not break down my big audacious goals into daily targets, review them every single day, and ensure that the minimum number of inputs were taking place to get our desired outputs.

Every once in awhile I would do these things, but I was not focused on them daily.

So that will be the first thing I change in 2016.

I've now calculated what our daily results need to be, and have worked backwards to determine the minimum number of inputs needed.

For example, I've calculated how many front-end units will we need to sell each day.

I've calculated how many events we'll need to do throughout the year, and how many event registrations we'll need to collect on each one.

I've calculated how many sales reps we'll need to hit these targets.

And just as important as having a daily plan of action, I'm also going to have 2 reviews per week with my CFO and our top sales managers, where we go through what our targets are, and whether we are on track to hit them.

I'm sure you've heard this before; but a rocket is off track over 90% of the time. It's continually being brought back on track by its navigation system.

Those 2 reviews I do per week will become my navigation system.

I strongly suggest you have your own navigation system in place.

To help you plan out 2016, and to set huge goals for your business results, I've invited long time friend and peak performance expert JT DeBolt to come train you this Tuesday, at 9pm EST.

The training is called: 3 Secrets To Making 2016 Your Best And Most Profitable Year Ever

You can register here: https://mobemarketplace.com/weekly-webinar

On a personal note, I first heard about JT back in 2009, when I was starting out with my first direct sales company. We were in the same company and he was one of the top earners there.

We didn't start working together till several years later, when I hired him to come host the 'Daily Power Up' calls.

He also emcees a lot of our MOBE Masterminds around the world - including the last one we did in Phuket, Thailand.

This man can help you choose high business goals for 2016, but more importantly he can help you achieve your high business goals.

12 months from now, you'll be looking back on 2016. Will you be satisfied with your results?

Attending this training will go a long way towards you being able to say YES.

Register here: https://mobemarketplace.com/weekly-webinar

Again it starts 9pm EST Tuesday night.

Talk soon,

Matt Lloyd

Subject: Hidden camera catches rare footage of my #1 lesson in business {Video}

Hey,

The most valuable lesson I have learned in the past 5 years of building an online business online, is that execution is king.

You can have the greatest ideas in the world... and all the courses under your belt - but if you can't take action and do the things that actually result in getting customers, you have no business.

When it comes to creating marketing (whether it's an email, sales letter, sales webinar, etc), a mentor or mine put it best when he said; 'good enough, is good enough.'

It's this idea of being ok with not having things perfect.

In my own case, I used to be the guy who wanted to have ALL the answers before ever pulling the trigger on anything.

For example: from early 2009 to 2010, I could never work up the nerve to do a simple webinar.

I'd been on other marketers webinars before. I'd bought products on their webinars before. I knew that eventually, I should start doing my own.

But, I had no clue how.

What software should I use? What sort of content should I prepare? How would I get people to actually show up? And how would I get people to buy whatever I was selling?

Finally I just decided to do my first one.

The rest is history. I've since sold millions of dollars on webinars, and in many cases they are thrown with little preparation.

Good enough is good enough.

At a recent seminar in Melbourne I did, I was showing the audience just how fast they too can do their own webinars and create big pay days.

My Camtasia webcam was left on, so I captured a good part of the segment on video:

[video]

The audio is not great, but it's the lesson that is important; floored execution is better than no execution at all.

In this case, I was showing them how to sell a course called 'Autoresponder Madness' (which just so happens to be the best course on email marketing available today).

The point I'm making is not that you should necessarily go and do a webinar.

It's that where you are today in your business (whether you run a 10m / year operation, or you are just beginning to learn internet marketing) is a direct result of how willing you are to execute on the things that bring you customers.

If you can find a way to speed that up - your business will start moving forwards a lot faster.

Hope that helps.

Talk soon,

Matt Lloyd

Subject: [Photo inside] How's this for a view?

I'm writing this email to you from my balcony here at the Barcelo Deluxe Resort, in the Dominican Republic.

It's not a bad view to have for the afternoon...

[video]

We're here for the Titanium Mastermind, which actually begins tonight.

We have close to 300 people flying in from all around the world, so it will be one of our bigger masterminds we've ever done.

Each person and their guest has invested 9,000 USD to come to this - so they are very serious about their marketing and business building education.

And they are in for an incredible few days with our trainers here, who I've hand picked myself.

To train at Titanium, you need to have accomplished amazing things in your own business, and be in a position to teach others how to do the same.

One of the trainers for example has sold over $150m worth of his own programs through direct mail.

Another, has sold over $4b worth of other people's products through TV infomercials.

We even have a famous hypnotist from Las Vegas (who'll also be doing a show and hypnotising some of our audience on the 2nd night!) who's helped clients all over the world reprogram their mind to achieve more wealth and get past any mental blocks they have in their business.

Anyway, one of the things I'll be stressing to each attendee in my opening session tomorrow is the futility of trying to implement everything they learn at this mastermind.

Instead, I'll be telling them to focus on implementing just a few key lessons that will have the biggest impact on their business.

I'm sure you've been to events before, where you took copious notes - pages of them - and then 2 months after you got home, you found that notepad laying around somewhere unopened, with none of the notes you took implemented.

I know I've done that many times myself.

So instead, I'll be stressing to them to focus on getting just 3 things from this mastermind.

3 big things... that will be worth far more than 9k to their business in the long term.

It could be a connection with a new key business partner...

It could be an idea for dramatically increasing sales...

It could be an experience - a conversation with an entrepreneur who's done over 8 figures in their business over a lunch, where they say something to you that causes a huge shift.

Whatever it is, they should focus on getting just 3 big things and fully implementing them - rather than a hundred small things they'll never implement.

If you attend live training events every once in a awhile, you should do the same.

This is a lesson I've learned the hard way over and over again.

The past few years when attending events I decided to instead focus on a few key things (to tell you the truth, I usually look for just ONE big major thing) - and it's done wonders for my business.

Example: one connection I got at a $4,000 mastermind in San Diego back in September has been worth over $3.5m in revenue for MOBE.

As far as ROIs come, they don't get much better than that.

So just remember my advice the next time you attend a live training event, and you'll get a lot more value from them.

Now, if you're wondering how you can get an invite to one of MOBE's future masterminds (we do them all over the world) the best way to find out more is to go through this program:

[video]

A lot of the photos you'll see on that page are also from previous masterminds we've done - as you can see, they are a lot of fun.

Ok, talk soon. I'm going to start getting ready for tonight.

Matt

.... **EMAIL EXAMPLE 8** ....

Subject: Mayweather and Pacquiao (and your business)

Hey,

You may or may not have any interest in the sport of boxing, but I'd be willing to bet you were aware of the big bout between Manny Pacquiao and Floyd Mayweather last night...

It's been all over the news recently - and the number of people who watched the fight was staggering.

After live gate and Pay Per View ticket sales, Mayweather will make close to 180 million dollars from it, and Pacquiao close to 120 million.

I ended up watching it in a bar in Phuket, Thailand at 10am in the morning as it was broadcast live.

Mayweather ended up winning on points, but some thought Pacquiao won (including himself).

But what really caught my attention were the reactions of people to it.

Suddenly people who know nothing about boxing became experts.

A drunken man sitting behind me in the bar was shouting his 'advice' to one of the boxers.

He knew he was right of course.

I cringed every time this guy opened his mouth - he was totally obnoxious. I felt like explaining to him why he did not know what he was talking about; but knew better.

Now, I myself am no expert on boxing.

But I have been doing it myself since the age of 17, on and off.

I've followed the sport fairly closely and I'm a fan of both Pacquaio and Mayweather for their raw talent and skill in the boxing ring.

In this case, I've watched many of each fighter's biggest fights several times...

I know enough about boxing to know what was really happening in the fight - and to immediately tell if someone else commenting has no idea what they are talking about.

People who've never boxed in their lives are suddenly giving advice on what each fighter could have done better.

And online, it was even worse.

Check your Facebook newsfeed and you'll see what I'm talking about.

***

So what does this have to do with marketing and your business?

Everything.

When it comes to the pursuit of mastery in any field - whether it's building a business, learning to generate traffic online, selling on the phone, or anything - you're going to be offered a lot of free advice.

You're going to get a lot of opinions.

People will happily give you their view and their advice, as if it's the absolute truth.

Some will do it with absolute conviction (these are the most dangerous).

It's fine to have an opinion of course, and everyone is entitled to one.

But when you're on the receiving end of someone's opinion or advice - you really need to be able to discern whether their opinion or advice should carry any real weight with it.

If you're new at marketing online - just be careful where you get your advice from.

Always question the source.

Do they have a motive for having a certain view ?

Do they have the results you aspire to have?

If they say they have the results, can you verify this to some extent? (at least half of the claims marketers make online are grossly exaggerated).

The great thing about the internet: freedom of publishing.

The bad thing about the internet: freedom of publishing.

You end up getting an ocean of unqualified opinions, and when you're reading those opinions trying to find the real answers, it can be very difficult to discern the qualified ones from the unqualified ones.

Most newer online marketers too easily accept what they view on the screen in front of them as being the truth.

Here's my advice: if you want to get ahead in this game, ignore 99% of the opinions and advice you get, period.

Especially when it comes to online marketing.

There's just so much garbage out there.

You can listen to the opinions of course when they are given with well meaning intentions.

Nod your head up and down politely as I often do when people give me business advice (yet have not built any significant business themselves).

But ignore most of the free advice you get.

If you want quality advice, then go find people who've achieved the results you aspire to - or have direct experience in the topic you want clarity on - and PAY them for it.

Free business advice is often worth what you pay for it; nothing.

Many times it's worth less than nothing.

It costs you money, because if you act on it you end up making the wrong decisions.

The best advice I've got and profited from, has being advice I paid large amounts of money for.

I've paid up to $10,000 for 8 hours of consulting before.

In one case, I paid that sum to the same company twice.

And it was worth every penny. Literally some of the best money I've ever spent.

So just remember this the next time you're reading something online about what it takes to do well in internet marketing...

If you have a comment on this (or the Mayweather Vs. Pacquiao fight) leave it HERE [facebook link] - I'm curious to hear your thoughts).

Talk soon,

Matt Lloyd

P.S.: Friends and family are often the worst offenders when it comes to giving bad business advice.

They mean well... but often have no experience in what they're talking about.

I had people in my direct family tell me that it was time to quit in late 2009 - that I was never going to make any money online.

By then I'd learned the lesson of choosing who you take advice from very carefully.

I chose to ignore them.

A couple years later, I came out with the MOBE License Rights Program.

A few months later, I remember reading a comment in forum about MOBE and our business model of 'licensing' core products that others could sell for 90% commissions.

A more experienced member of the forum gave a lengthy review of why that business model would never work and how no one would pay for such a thing.

Since then, many thousands of people have got started with this program and it's one of our best sellers.

PPS. It's been nearly a week since I sent a live broadcast email out to you... I usually try to stay in touch every couple days, so you may have been wondering what happened...

I've actually been pretty busy - traveling to Singapore last week to speak at the Home Business Summit, then on to Kota Kinabalu in Malaysia for a few nights (where we are hosting our July Platinum Mastermind), and then I stayed another 4 nights in Phuket, Thailand (the destination of another upcoming Mastermind).

Now I'm back home.

We were shooting 2 new promo videos for these masterminds and choosing the final resorts we'll be doing them at.

I can't wait to show you these new videos... you are going to love them.

Get access to the ultimate HTAM (High Ticket Affiliate Marketing) system, which pays you up to $13,500 per sale at **www.fivefigureaffiliatemarketing.com**. You will also be assigned a personal HTAM coach, who will walk you through a simple, 21 step training program that shows you how to get started.

You'll see some of the activities you'll get to experience when coming to these masterminds… including watching a man get in a snake pit with 4 Cobra snakes (I also climbed in for a brief 30 seconds, just for the video).

You'll see the shooting range you'll be able to go to and fire a pump action shotgun.

Then you'll see me getting shot by one of my staff members with a paintball gun…

(did I mention some of these activities are optional, and you can choose which ones to do?)

You'll see me getting up close to a giant lizard that was literally the same size as me…

…riding elephants, and zip lining at high speeds from one island to another.

And then seeing a live Thai Kickboxing show, working out with a monkey, and getting up close to the biggest buddha statue I've ever seen (literally as high as 3 houses stacked on each other).

All of this is coming soon over the next few weeks - look out for my emails.

·· **EMAIL EXAMPLE 9** ··

Subject: Case Study: How I manage a virtual staff of over 100 people around the world…

Hey,

So I'm back on the road. Right now it's 6am and I'm in a London airport coffee shop, after sitting through a 14 hour flight. Shortly, I'll be boarding a 10 hour flight to Charlotte, then a few more hours to Florida.

I'm going there to attend a 3 day training event for ceo's and company owners on how to scale company's faster and more effectively.

No matter what level of success you reach in business, I'm a big believer in continually investing in your own education. It's the only way you'll get to the next level.

After that event I fly 35 hours to Sydney, to put on the first Super Charge Summit of 2016 for our MOBE affiliates, where I'll be training them on how to dramatically increase their earnings.

Then it's to Hong Kong for a night to open a new company, and then finally... I fly home.

It's going to be a grueling trip. But don't feel too sorry for me; I love this life.

I especially love training our affiliates and helping them succeed.

When MOBE began it's affiliate program way back in early 2011, it was a big deal to see one of them make a sale.

Back then, the commissions were much smaller (they started out at $48), and I'd call back every single affiliate who made a sale. I think I was more excited about it than they were!

Fast forward to today, and we've now paid out $49,690,371.05 in total commissions.

I'm just as grateful for the thousands of affiliates we have these days (including the ones who are yet to make their first sale) as I was way back in 2011.

One of our first 'super affiliates' was a guy called John Chow, who as of today just crossed over $2,000,000 with our affiliate program.

He came on board back in September of 2012, after we met at a mastermind event in San Diego.

I was talking to John the other night on Skype and he asked me a question about building large companies through a virtual staff.

His question was: "How do you manage a staff of over 100 people, when they are scattered throughout the world?"

Even though you might not yet have hired your first staff member (or first few), you'll get tremendous value from watching my answer below in this video: Watch Here.

[video]

At some point if you want to keep scaling your business and breaking through new revenue ceilings, you've got to build a team. (without my team behind me, MOBE wouldn't be a 1/100th of it's current size today).

Also, while we're on the topic of building teams - don't feel you need to have 100s of staff to make a lot of money online. John has less than 5 staff in his company, (which he talks about at the end of the video) and yet he still makes millions.

Part of the reason he's been able to make the kind of money he has with so few staff, is because he promotes other companies like mine as an affiliate.

This way, he doesn't have to create the products, put on the live events, manage entire teams of sales staff, deal with thousands of support tickets every month, and have staff overheads that cost over 100k a month.

He lets people like me manage all of that, and he focuses on one thing; sending targeted traffic to our offers.

My company then goes to work on converting his traffic, and getting him paid.

One of the hot offers that is currently doing really well for John, is our new 'Internet Funnel System.

This $49 course shows the client how to get involved in 'high ticket affiliate marketing' (the same that John does) so you can make larger affiliate commissions. Right up to 10k per sale.

A very large % of John's 2m has come from promoting high ticket programs.

Think about it for a second; if you're goal is 10k / month, do you think it's easier to find 1,000 customers each month who will buy a $10 ebook? Or, do you think it's easier to find just ONE customer who will pay 10k for a high value program?

The latter is much easier.

And this course will teach you how.

[video]

I'll be in touch soon - I'm not sure which country I'll be in, but till we talk next... keep scaling your business.

Talk soon,

Matt

How to Make Big Commissions By Simply Giving Away Copies Of The Limitless Book...

Congratulations - you've made it to the end of this book.

I trust that you can now see an entirely new and exciting future for yourself, in the world of High Ticket Affiliate Marketing (HTAM). Now comes the most important step to making money with what you've learned; taking action.

The first thing you need to do is join the MOBE HTAM program. It won't take you more than 3 minutes to do this.

Just go to **www.fivefigureaffiliatemarketing.com** and complete the steps.

Once you've done that, you're in a position to now start making commissions by sending traffic (i.e. eyeballs) in front of different MOBE offers. The book you just read is an example of a MOBE offer.

You may have noticed that on every second page there was a link directing you back to the MOBE website where you can sign up to get on our email list.

Well, as a marketing company, one of the things we'll do to any new subscribers is market to them. We'll find different ways we can help them in their business, and, offer them our products.

If you send us one of those subscribers, we'll make sure you get paid commissions on everything they buy. All you need to do, is hand out copies of Limitless to good, qualified prospects. MOBE then takes care of the rest and you'll get paid.

How to get Started?

To do this, you'll need to order a stack of Limitless books. We'll have our printer custom print your own unique affiliate link throughout the pages of these books, so that all the sales get tracked back to you (and you get paid).

You can get started with just 50 books. These won't take long to hand out, and as soon as you get paid some commissions, you can then reinvest some of those earnings back into getting more books, and scale up (just like I taught you).

To get your first box of Limitless books, simply go to www.MOBE.com/limitless-books

Make Money Giving Away Copies Of Limitless in 3 Easy Steps:

Step 1: Get a box of Limitless books which will be sent to you in the mail by going to: www.MOBE.com/limitless-books

Step 2: Start handing out copies of Limitless to people you know who are open to starting a business (or already in business) and encouraging them to read it.

Step 3: When they go to the link inside the book and buy something from MOBE, you'll get paid your commission. The more they buy, the more you get paid.

This is the exact same High Ticket Affiliate Program that's paid out over $51 million so far.

Take action now, and I look forward to hearing about your results at a MOBE live event in the future.

ABOUT THE AUTHOR
Matt Lloyd

Matt Lloyd is CEO and Founder of MOBE (My Online Business Education), an award winning Education Company which has impacted students on a global scale.

MOBE's mission is to be the number one training resource in the world for small business owners and entrepreneurs.

Like many who make the transition from employee to business owner, Matt at first struggled. In his first few years of building an online marketing business he faced a steep learning curve.

But through investing heavily in his own business education, and by taking massive action, he went on to make his first million dollars on the internet by age 25.

By age 28, his companies had grossed over $100 million in sales.

Now Matt focuses all of this time on giving back to other aspiring entrepreneurs, and creating education programs which teach others how to effectively build and grow their businesses.

He spends approximately one third of his year traveling the world, hosting and teaching his live workshops, seminars and exclusive masterminds.

You can learn more about how MOBE can help you build your business at www.mobe.com

The MOBE High Ticket Affiliate Program is the world's best HTAM system that pays you up to $13,500 per sale!

Backend high-ticket sales are made FOR YOU: MOBE does the work and deposits commissions directly into your bank account twice a month!

PLUS ... you get a **personal coach** that will walk you through a simple 21-step training program on how to make your first BIG commission (even if you have zero computer skills!)

90% of the work required to run a business is Done For You:

- ✓ No products to create
- ✓ No fulfillment or customer service
- ✓ No payment processing
- ✓ No website design or hosting
- ✓ No sales presentations or funnels to create
- ✓ No selling in person or over the phone

... It's all Done For You!

Join today at: **www.fivefigureaffiliatemarketing.com**